OVER COME

*Say Goodbye to Shame,
Get Past Your Past &
Win Out Over Temptation*

JOSHUA FINLEY

DEDICATION

I dedicate this book to our two sons, Judah and Jesse.
After your innocence has been challenged on all sides, may your
purity remain. Victory is your lot and freedom is your portion.
May you never forget that you live under the smile of heaven.
And may this promise become your reality:
"The pure in heart will see God."
– Jesus in Matthew 5:8

CONTENTS

7	**ENDORSEMENTS**
13	**FOREWORD**
17	**INTRODUCTION**

23 · **Chapter 1:**
The Blessing of Boundaries

35 · **Chapter 2:**
Sweat the Small Stuff

55 · **Chapter 3:**
The Slippery Slope

75 · **Chapter 4:**
The Real Problem with Porn

95 · **Chapter 5:**
Shame OFF You!

117 · **Chapter 6:**
Winning Within: Character Stronger Than Our Hormones

139 · **Chapter 7:**
Kingdom Community

153 · **Chapter 8:**
The Truth About You

175 · **Chapter 9:**
Thinking for a Change

195 · **Chapter 10:**
Afterwards: The Battle You Fight After the Battle You Win

217 · **ACKNOWLEDGMENTS**
219 · **ENDNOTES**

CONTENTS

ENDORSEMENTS

FOREWORD

INTRODUCTION

Chapter 1

Chapter 2
Samson and Saul

Chapter 3
The Slippery Slope

Chapter 4

Chapter 5

Chapter 6

Chapter 7

Chapter 8

Chapter 9

Chapter 10

ACKNOWLEDGEMENTS

ENDNOTES

ENDORSEMENTS

"*Overcome* is a biblically framed playbook for winning, resting, and living your best life now. Joshua's highly developed executive life coaching and communication skills enable him to weave inspiring stories and powerful illustrations that empower the reader. I have had the joy and privilege of watching this beloved son live these dynamic life-giving principles for decades. This book is a practical manual and a transformative leadership tool."

ERIC PEOPLES
Lead Pastor of Legacy Church (Farmington, CT)
Co-founder of The Mastermind Experience

"If you can win the private war against the lust of the flesh you will eventually walk in the rarified air among other spiritual giants. I'm absolutely convinced of that. Too many have shipwrecked their life and family because they became lax in the disciplines that develop moral excellence. Joshua Finley comes alongside the reader and offers lifestyle practices that introduce you to victory—sustainable victory with your sexuality. *Overcome* is one of those books you'll read and pass along to others who long to be victors in their private world."

DAVID D. IRELAND, PH.D.
Lead Pastor | Author of *One in Christ* and *Raising a Child Who Prays*

"It is one thing to simply live saved by grace. It is another thing to live saved by grace in a victorious and abundant manner. My dear friend Joshua Finley unpacks the nuts and bolts on how you can live this excellent and victorious walk with Christ here on earth. This book will give you a greater understanding and clarity on how you can overcome the baggage that keeps us from living the next level God has for you!"

TEOFILO HAYASHI
Founder of Dunamis Movement (São Paolo, Brazil) | Co-leader of The Send

"Every thinking person desires at heart to be an overcomer. Nothing succeeds without a plan. Titles abound, telling us how to win in life. There must be, however, more than a desire; there must be a guide. Joshua Finley has skillfully constructed a grid for such an overcoming life and invites the reader to deal with the negatives, believe the positives and engage with Jesus Christ."

JACK TAYLOR
President of Dimensions Ministries

"My friend Joshua Finley has written a book that every heart needs to know. A must read for anyone called to reign in life!"

LEIF HETLAND
President of Global Mission Awareness | Author of *Called to Reign*

"Sin is our deadliest enemy. Thankfully, we don't have to battle alone. Through his exceptional gift of storytelling, Joshua skillfully gives us practical ways to overcome that he's proven himself through his own journey. May this book guide your steps into the victory of Christ!"

BOB SORGE
Author of *A Covenant with My Eyes*

"I believe Joshua Finley is one of the most significant, grounded, expansive Christian leaders in this generation. I so appreciate his profound insight and humility as he takes the reader on a journey through the experiences which have created his history in God. *Overcome* reveals the beautiful revelation of the power of God's grace in the midst of our humanity. Joshua marks a clear plan for anyone desiring to build strongly in God. I highly recommend stepping into the pages of Joshua's transparent work which reveals practical steps to help live a more wholly holy life."

ROBERT STEARNS
Bishop of The Tabernacle (Buffalo, NY) | Founder of Eagles' Wings

"*Overcome* is filled with wisdom that's relevant for God's people today—for such a time as this. Joshua Finley's writing is a beautiful balance of the compassion of a loving father and the authority of a coach. The freedom Joshua has encountered in his own life has opened a floodgate for him to lead and teach others in the way of freedom. His words are gold, his wisdom is a gift, and I'm grateful to call him a friend."

WADE HASKINS
Lead Pastor of Freedom Church (Bel Air, MD)

"Joshua Finley is one of the most outstanding young leaders I have personally ever worked with. In his book *Overcome* he shares the Biblical principles that have enabled him to shake off the hindrances that have paralyzed his generation. You too can overcome through applying the truths that he shares."

MICHAEL CAVANAUGH
Founding Pastor of Elim Gospel Church (Lima, NY) | President Emeritus of Elim Bible Institute & College | Author of *The Power & Purpose of Singleness*

"Since the inception of The Fall in Genesis 3:7, the catastrophic collapse of God's human creation has never stopped struggling in what would appear to seem like endless areas of our lives. In his book *Overcome*, Joshua Finley has brilliantly and uniquely tapped into the epicenter of both the depth of our fallen human condition and the hope of a stronger and more vibrant life in Jesus. Providing practical, understandable and powerful tools, Joshua hands us the antidote so we can; '…have life and [have] it more abundantly.'"

FRED ANTONELLI, PH.D., LPCMH
Therapist & Founder/Director of Life Counseling Center |
Author of *Struggling Well*

"If you are looking for a book that walks you through life's temptations, struggles and difficulties, then Josh Finley's book, *Overcome*, is the book to read. This book will give you the tools you need to live life more abundantly. Not only will you say goodbye to sin, shame and your strongholds, but you will be strengthened as you walk in the newness of life. Reading this book will encourage tremendous Kingdom advancement in you and in the legacy you leave."

CHRIS BALL
President of Elim Fellowship

"*Overcome* is a rare and welcome gift. In an age where Christian teaching often requires one to make a false choice between the ideas of Grace and Truth, Josh Finley has put a stake in the ground, boldly claiming that we must choose both! To read *Overcome* is to engage on a journey of freedom from shame and sin by embracing the liberating power of Jesus' relentless love and unstoppable grace!"

JOHN CARTER
Senior Pastor of Abundant Life Christian Center (Syracuse, NY) | Founder
of Mercy Works | Author of *The Transformed Life*

"Joshua Finley is my personal example of how to live the overcoming life as I've watched him walk it out for almost 20 years. With vulnerability and wisdom, in *Overcome* he lays out a blueprint for how to build a life of excellence and integrity. This handbook on practical holiness is a must read for every person who wants to rise above sin and shame."

TOBY CAVANAUGH
Co-founder of Campus Target | Founder of Ephesus School of Ministry

"Too often the Church's answer to overcoming sin has been that we must simply "pray more." While prayer is one of the most powerful tools you can use to find freedom, it is an encounter with God combined with practical Bible-based tools that will help you walk in victory over sin on a daily basis. Through entertaining storytelling and powerful teaching of God's Word, Joshua Finley walks you through insightful tools for avoiding sin, along with truths from Scripture that will transform the way you think about living an overcoming life. As someone who has sat under his teaching and seen his character and integrity up close, I highly recommend you read *Overcome* to learn more about the grace and power of God in your life!"

CHRIS ZEIGLER
Executive Director of BASIC College Ministries

FOREWORD

There aren't a lot of pastors who will talk about sex from their pulpit, let alone fly another communicator across the country to spend a whole two days unpacking the controversial topic. But that's precisely what Josh Finley did three years ago.

As I entered the green room, before the evening event, my mind was busy preparing. I was thinking about the room full of young people coming in ready to tackle the subject of healthy sexuality. I was currently serving as the Director of Moral Revolution, a nonprofit ministry based in Redding, CA. Our focus was simple; create resources to help the church talk about sex, purity and a lifestyle of freedom.

Upon entering, Pastor Joshua Finley immediately greeted my husband and me. He was at the helm of this rural, thriving, college community. His warmth and energy made our conversation natural. Introducing him to our four young sons, he apologized for the absence of his wife. Her dad was dying of cancer, and she was savoring every moment with him.

Ben and I liked Pastor Josh right away. His authenticity was palpable, with his intellect peeking through our various range of topics. We quickly struck up a friendship, a friendship which has continued to this very day.

It was very apparent Josh had the heart to help others understand where they struggled. Those places weren't life sentences but rather a genesis of God's grace and healing. Why else would he fly the six of us to his small town to speak in front of his congregation? Why would he fund an event so families and young people could learn about this vital topic? Josh had the heart to change people's lives. I don't think that's far-fetched from many people in leadership today. But the difference isn't always about a heart to do it, that's natural. Instead, it's in creating and investing in opportunities to encounter truth. I believe this book does exactly what he was doing years ago — creating space to invest his words in unpacking seemingly complicated topics. The church is ready for this message.

I grew up with learning issues. A perfect cocktail of dyslexia and comprehension difficulties made learning excruciating. Born in a high performing and prestigious family, I didn't think I had anything to give the world. Spending many years as a young woman telling God He'd picked the wrong person. I wasn't His best choice; in fact, I felt like more of a liability. It took me many years, and many tears to begin to discover my real purpose. But as I continued my journey, I began to see my mandate was to help unpack complicated topics in the church. I'd felt so lost learning, that I didn't want anyone to feel that way in their walk with Christ. I'm obsessed with helping others understand the truth. Now I spend every day doing this exact thing.

Josh is doing this exact thing in these pages. These words are an easy read but don't let that cause you to second-guess the quality and power of his writings. They are rich with meaning, dripping with truth. His stories immediately pulled me in. I caught myself laughing as I read through his moments as a young man. I'm sure all of us can think of a time in our lives where our immaturity caught up with us. There were parts I immediately thought, "I need to remember this... that's exactly how to stay free."

Josh's honesty was refreshing. Inspiring. He's not speaking down to us but instead encouraging each of us to join him on the journey into freedom. It's evident; he's passionate about living free from shame and guilt. It's even more apparent he doesn't want to go there alone, but he wants to take his generation with him.

I'm confident the book you're holding in your hands didn't just come from a man who sat down to write a book. It came from a man who had purposed to live his life in full freedom and radical authenticity. His words may come easy, but I can assure you, the price for the revelation and vulnerability has not. It would be natural to be inspired by Josh's life, but if we use the tools and truth he's laid out for each of us, we can be equipped and empowered to live a life which overcomes.

To Those Who Overcome,

HAVILAH CUNNINGTON
Founder of Truth to Table
Author of *Stronger Than the Struggle*

INTRODUCTION

Freedom. Victory over sin. I believe it is a passion of God's for His people to be free. He actually designed us to live in freedom. It is a passion of mine as well. Maybe it's because in the young stages of life—what some call the "warrior stage"—my battles related to the war within, personal spiritual warfare. As a young man, my mind was imprinted with battles- a war between sin and a deep desire to please God and not blow it. I sought the Lord a lot in those years, and He taught me some powerful things. He's still teaching me how to fight my battles.

Formulas can be dangerous: what works for one person may not work exactly the same way for another. Nevertheless, the Bible is true, and there are principles for conquering sin that really work. The best part about the Gospel is that it's true and it works! As you take hold of God's promises and keep your eyes on Jesus, the enemy will continue to lose territory in your life. You may lose a skirmish here or there, but temptation cannot defeat you in the long haul. You will look back one day and say, "I used to be a slave to that, but I'm not anymore!"

I never wanted my first published book to be about overcoming sin and winning in times of temptation. I guess I did not want people to think I was a pervert or that this was my life message. "I've got so many other topics and books in me LORD!" That was my rationale. That was my excuse. Clearly "image-maintenance" was one of my idols I needed to lay down. I knew in my head that people connect far more over our struggles than over our successes. I just wanted people to be able to connect and relate to someone else's struggles while I shared my successes-classic Enneagram three dilemma.

Here's how it happened. I taught a message series on these topics and began to see profound freedom come to the lives of our church family. To be honest, the inspiration to put these teachings in print came from a husband who was battling to keep his marriage of forty-eight years. He and his wife were temporarily separated. He strongly encouraged me, "This content has brought me so much freedom! You have to get this teaching out to people who really need breakthrough from God's Word!" I was glad he was encouraged. I was ever more elated when I received an invitation to he and his wife's fiftieth anniversary!

> **"Temptation is actually a test of relationship more than discipline."**
>
> CHRIS HODGES

I was still not convinced I needed to write a book, but something happened. Something happened inside of me. I felt a strong nudge from the Holy Spirit. My vision grew for people getting free. I stopped worrying about what people might think of me as we journey through these difficult topics. It is good to be self-aware, but it can be paralyzing to become overly self-conscious. Self-awareness is a growing understanding of how you think and operate in order that you might serve others. Self-awareness enlarges your world. Self-consciousness can become an over fixation on your own internal world and perspective. Self-consciousness can shrink your world and cause you to be stingy with your resources, revelation and experiences. Needless to say, the LORD had to work me over pretty good to get this book to print. Yet, I want you to hear this. Every bit of my struggle to live this out, to write this out and to get this out was worth it. Your freedom is worth it. Thank you for the honor of coming alongside of you in your battle.

The life of Freedom is based on relationship. A passionate "yes" to Jesus is always stronger than a disciplined "no" towards sin. Sometimes people feel as if they have to say a million "no's" when it comes to temptation. There certainly is a great deal of truth to that. However, I want to help you find your most powerful "yes" to God.

I love these words of David concerning the Messiah:

> *The Lord said to my Lord, "Sit at My right hand, till I make Your enemies Your footstool." (Psalm 110:1 NKJV)*

This verse is quoted six times in the New Testament. That fact alone should cause us to pause and ask, "Why?" The point in history in which we currently live is wrapped up in that four-letter word "till." We are in that time when Jesus is seated at the Father's right hand until all the enemies of God are put under His feet. One day, He will stand and be sent to us for His glorious returning. Until then, believers are seated in Christ at the right hand (see Ephesians 2:6), and we are the ones that God is using to put His enemies under His footstool. Since we are His Body, it is through our lives that He overcomes. His victory has now become our inheritance. Our victory will soon become His reward and glory.

"**Every decision that you and I make eventually becomes a story that we will tell.**"

ANDY STANLEY

01

THE BLESSING
OF BOUNDARIES

When I was young growing up, I was terribly afraid of small spaces. I had a fear of being trapped. I wouldn't go so far as to say that I was claustrophobic, but … I was probably claustrophobic!

My fears were so bad that I was notorious for ruining every hide-and-seek game my five siblings and I ever played. I remember one time we were playing, and I had one of the best hiding places in the house, back in the dark corner of a linen closet in the hallway. Nobody was going to find me. I was sure to win. As I tried to wait calmly in the blackness, with confidence that I had this game in the bag, the fear of tight spaces began to come over me. It escalated to the point that I suddenly kicked open the door and burst out into the open visibility of the hallway.

I hated being trapped in small spaces. While that can seem like a minute issue, it translated into something much bigger in my life and a pattern developed. As I grew up, it wasn't simply that I had a fear of small spaces. I began to see every boundary around me as something that I must push against, because I thought that I was being trapped. People who feel trapped can learn to live with a limited perspective. I even began to mistakenly believe the lie that if I remained submissive in the will of God, I would be trapped.

This all really came to light on a mission trip in the summer between my junior and senior year in high school. On the way home from our trip to Scotland, we had a layover at the Reykjavík-Keflavík International Airport in Iceland. Although our whole team was exhausted, we were more excited by the opportunity to see Iceland. Who ever gets a chance to see a place like Iceland, I thought.

Not long into our exploration of this land filled with volcanic rock, our pastor announced that he was taking us to a natural hot springs called Blue Lagoon, located in a huge, old lava field. Picture a beautiful lake that is turned into a hot tub, water temperatures in the swimming area averaging around 100 degrees! Steam lifts off the seawater in the most picturesque, peaceful way. It is a geothermal oasis of relaxation—the hottest hot tub you've ever been in at any time in your whole life, formed from natural elements, in one of the starkest landscapes imaginable.

As our tour bus slowed to a stop, none of us could wait to hop out and run into the changing rooms to put on our bathing suits. We hurried and jumped into the seawater hot springs for what I was sure would be the most exciting swimming experience of my life. But I had never been in a hot spring before. I didn't understand what happens in the human body. Your heart rate starts to slow down. You try to swim, but it's hard to freestyle swim more than a few strokes without being out of breath. For safety, there were buoys dispersed throughout the area for resting, because they know that you can't swim endlessly in a hot spring or you'll drown!

I also noticed that there was a rope set around the hot spring as a boundary. The water we were swimming in inside of the rope boundary was so warm and inviting that there was really no need to leave it. Outside of the boundary, however, I noticed the steam lifting up off the water even more beautifully, even more dense and thick. Inside of my adventurous, 16-year-old brain, I thought it only seemed logical that the water outside the rope boundary must be more awesome than the water we were enjoying inside of the boundary. I used my best skills of influence in a vain attempt to coax my friends to join me in crossing the seemingly unnecessary barrier to a better life. They wouldn't budge, except to follow me to the last buoy closest to the boundary. Using that last buoy as a basecamp from which to set out, I determined to explore the restricted waters on the other side of the rope.

It was a bit of a distance from the last buoy to the hazard rope, but with all of my breath and Olympian-like strength, I pushed out to the rope and grabbed a hold to take one last breath on the boring side. Ignoring the posted "Hazard" and "Stay Away!" signs, I threw my legs across the boundary rope to the other side. I couldn't wait to see what it felt like! My friends watched with excitement as their buddy dared the elements and abandoned the rules to go where no man had gone before (although someone must have, because they knew to post the signs there).

What happened next was that out of my innermost being flowed the loudest shrill you've ever heard, worse than any scream you would hear at a junior high girls' slumber party.

I was in pain! The water there was scalding! My high-pitched cry pierced through the air and frightened my friends who waited at the buoy, unsure what had happened or what to do at the sound of my wail. As quickly as I could and without any strength left, I stroked back to the buoy, gasping for air amid my own shrieks. I hurriedly made my way out of the water to examine the skin and assess the damages, certain my leg hair had melted off in the scalding treatment it had received. Fortunately, my skin and leg hair fared much better than my ego!

Underlying this traumatic encounter was the real problem: I didn't trust that the people who laid out the boundary rope and markers had my best interest in mind. I thought something good on the other side of the boundary was being withheld from my enjoyment.

WHAT DO YOU BELIEVE ABOUT BOUNDARIES?

How often do we do things like that in our lives, not trusting the boundaries that someone set in place for us? It is so easy for this to happen—in relationship to our parents, to the police, to other authority figures in our lives, even with God! When you and I don't trust and honor the boundary lines that have been put in our lives, bad things happen.

Even King David had to learn this valuable lesson. He had something to say about this in Psalm 16, where he wrote: *"Lord, apart from you I have no good thing [...] the boundary lines have fallen for me in pleasant places; surely I have a delightful inheritance."* And then he went on to say, *"in fact, in your presence is fullness of joy and at your right hand are the greatest pleasures for my life"* (Verses 2,6, and 11, New International Version). David tapped into something so important in this passage. He had learned how to embrace boundaries and to actually believe that when he did, God's blessing would come.

Do you believe that in the core of your being? Deep down, do you believe that God has more for you than anyone can ever offer you and that no one else can take it away? Satan's oldest trick in the book is to try to tempt us into reaching for something that is beyond the boundary. It can even be the "right thing" but in the wrong way or at the wrong time! You know that even the right thing at the wrong time brings disaster. Adam and Eve reached for the fruit. "Just stay within this one boundary," God said. I think of David reaching for the beautiful woman Bathsheba who was not his, a disastrous decision that resulted in the death of a child and some of his closest, most courageous friends and defenders. His decision brought years of violence and heartache to his family. Eventually, he had to get to a place where he understood that the boundary lines of God are pleasant. Life changes you when you come to that transformational truth and you embrace those boundaries.

RICHES OR BAGGAGE?

Proverbs 10:22 says that when God blesses you, "it makes one rich," and I have discovered that when He blesses you, He makes you rich like nobody else can. In fact, the second half of that verse spells it out like this: not only does His blessing make you personally a very wealthy person, but "He adds no sorrow to it."

Isn't that an incredible picture? Every time we give into a temptation to go out beyond the will of God and reach for something outside of the boundaries, purposes, and Word of God, even something we think will be a "blessing" that will add to our lives, it always comes back to hurt us. Yet when we trust and believe and wait patiently for God to bless us, He adds no sorrow to it. Every time I step out of the Lord's covering and boundaries, there is nothing there but bondage and baggage.

The most harmful and tragic decisions of my life up to this point occurred when I stepped outside of the boundaries that God had set for me in His love. My mistake was that I did not believe His boundaries fell for me in "pleasant places" and that He had a great inheritance for me, inside the boundaries.

It is belief in a lie that is at the heart of our errors, and it can manifest in so many areas of our lives. Boundaries are important in finances, for instance—how we use a credit card, manage our cravings to buy more things, make borrowing decisions, and weigh job opportunities that come our way. When we try to make things happen outside of God's will, it will always lead to financial bondage. The worst financial decisions of my life have always occurred when I've stepped over God's boundaries and wisdom.

Sexuality is another key area where understanding God's perimeters is critical. Giving up my virginity in a high school relationship was the worst mistake of my life! Had I known what God was preparing for me and had I believed that He wasn't keeping something from me but was, instead, preserving something for me, there is no way that I would have overstepped that boundary and cashed in my virginity. Nobody took that sexual purity from me and nobody can; I chose to lay my virginity down and stepped over a boundary line. The baggage I picked up in doing so was a weight God never intended for me to carry. We pick up shame when we step over boundaries. Had I believed and known the truth, I would have made a different decision entirely.

27

DECISIONS RESULT IN STORIES

Andy Stanley said it so well: "Every decision that you and I make eventually becomes a story that we will tell." Some stories we tell are stories we are proud of. We could tell them at parties, tell friends, share them as testimonies of God's goodness and kindness. Then there are other stories, however, that we are ashamed of. They are the stories of unnecessary pain and hardship that our actions and choices brought upon ourselves. God, thankfully, has the power to turn them into a testimony in His redeeming grace should we give them over to Him, but they are nonetheless stories that didn't need to be written.

Ask yourself the questions: What kind of stories do you want to tell when you are introduced to your future spouse? What kind of stories do you want to tell your children and grandchildren? Since every decision you make now becomes a story you will tell in the future, what kind of story do you want to tell when you look them in the face, eye to eye?

GETTING REAL ABOUT THE "MOMENT OF THE MAYBE"

A friend of mine obtained a rescue dog that was a few years old and already had a mind of its own. My friend installed an invisible fence, which worked great for a couple of weeks, until a neighbor called to say that the dog had treed his terrified cat. From that time on, the dog decided that ignoring the warning beep of the collar and the impending pain of electric shock was worth experiencing the temporary thrill of chasing cats, even though the poor dog never was able to catch the object of his chase.

That's kind of how sin works: there is a "promise" that is elusive, and there is real pain. But like the collar that beeps a warning not to go beyond the boundaries of the invisible fence, the Holy Spirit can be trusted to alert you when you near God's boundaries. When temptation comes to call you beyond that fence, you will sense the internal governing of the Spirit sending that beeping sound to your conscience.

After the enemy tempted Jesus in Luke 4, the Bible says that he left Jesus to come back again at an opportune time (Luke 4:13). This tells me that there are certain times, environments, and situations where we are more susceptible to temptation and other situations when the enemy is not even going to even try us. The enemy wanted Jesus to find His security (turning stones into bread), His safety (jumping off a cliff to be rescued by angels) and His significance (bow to the enemy and receive the Kingdoms of this world) in a source other than His father. The enemy will seek to get us to make those same exchanges.

So, what about those vulnerable or opportune times? What about that moment when the "maybe" question hits you, like, "Maybe the grass really is greener over there on the other side?" (By the way, have you ever noticed that when you climb across a fence into a greener pasture, the reason it appears visibly taller and greener is because there are lots of manure piles, which you could not see before? Or the grass isn't even real-it's turf!) Temptation to step outside the boundary always looks like a good deal! It never looks like it will hurt. It's the nature of the beast. Temptation always seems tempting! God isn't trying to withhold good things from us. The tempter is just trying to hurt us by making sin look so good but no one views sin the same after committing it.

Satan's the master bad check writer. Although his account is completely empty, he writes us large checks with things like "pride," "lust," "greed," written on them. He tells us there is more to cash in on in life than we are experiencing right now. But no matter how good or enticing the offer seems, the check will always bounce. Satan, the ways of the world, and the lusts of the flesh have nothing to offer you.

H.A.L.T.

What I'm about to share is both practical and powerful. Mentors of mine have been talking about this principle for years and it is so, so true. Keep in mind the word "H.A.L.T."

> ## "Your emotions are indicators, not dictators."
>
> BENNY PEREZ

H – Hungry
A – Angry
L – Lonely
T – Tired

If I am dominated by any of the four feelings listed above, I am more susceptible to give myself to something that is outside the will of God. This is because I will be acting on the appetites of my emotions or flesh rather than being governed by God's Spirit. My encouragement to you is the same as my mentors': when these types of emotions are hitting you strongly, step back from making any major decisions. HALT. As Mike Murdock once said, "Tired eyes rarely see a bright future."

Sometimes it's easy to think, "If I don't feel it, I can't do it (in regards to honoring God or saying no to sin.) I don't want to be a hypocrite." You're not a hypocrite, you're a human! Just remember this life-changing truth from Chris Hodges: "Choices lead, feelings follow."

FEED WHAT?

In the moment of the maybe, I also want to remind myself some words from Frank Damazio, "What I feed will live and what I starve will die!" This is always true. If you struggle with alcohol, there are situations that feed the temptation and others that starve it. Certain types of music can feed unhealthy mood swings in some. A sentimental journey through old photographs of past girlfriends or boyfriends can feed the renewal of unhealthy relationships out of the past and weaken current life-giving relationships that require a commitment in the present. If you struggle with a pornography addiction you cannot deal with that issue casually. If you deal with sin casually, you are more likely to become a casualty.

Here is the great news: grace is more powerful than sin! The grace of God empowers you and me to live out the truth of God and the will of God. The word "overcome" means to overwhelm or overpower something you are struggling with. The grace of God on your life literally overwhelms the sin in your life. We can all relate to Adam and Eve who ate of the tree of the knowledge of good and evil. Since then, we've joined the entire human race in proving that KNOWING what is right and wrong is POWERLESS to help us live right. The "want to" is much stronger than the "know how". Yet, embracing God's grace is more than POWERFUL enough to keep me within the boundaries of His truth.

And what if I fail? Failure is never fatal, because God is the God of another chance (He's not the God of a "second chance" as some say; He's the God of another chance…and another… and another…). So, when we feel like, "I don't know if I can do this. I've got this habitual sin or addiction," and other people may not even be aware of it, it's easy to believe that, "I'm going to be trapped into this small, dark or secret space for the rest of my life." I want you to know that this thought is a lie! You can be free. The grace of God is more powerful than whatever you are facing, and your past does not dictate what your future experience will be.

I have no doubt that if David were joining you and I in this conversation right now, after living a life of the good, the bad, and the ugly, he'd say, "The boundaries God has set in place to keep and to bless your life have actually fallen in very pleasant places. And God has an amazing inheritance for you." The Lord has more for you than anyone else can ever offer you, and nobody else can ever take it away. Embrace your boundaries. Don't fear being trapped in the will of God, and remember that God is not keeping something from you. He is preserving something *for* you.

"What I feed will live, and what I starve will die."

_____

FRANK DAMAZIO

02

SWEAT THE SMALL STUFF

Both of my parents worked during my childhood, so for a season I would spend the mornings at my grandparents' house. I would hang out with them and watch some episodes of the Brady Bunch (growing up in the 80s was great!) or other family shows on TV, and then they would send me to the afternoon session of kindergarten.

One morning while I was at my grandparents watching TV, I found this irritating little string hanging from my new jeans. As any little five or six year old would do, I began pulling on that string hoping to break it off. When the string wouldn't break, I just thought, *Let me pull harder.* The string grew longer and longer, but it would not separate from my pant leg. This may not have normally posed a real problem except that the string that I was pulling on was part of the inseam of my jeans that was stitched around my inner thigh and zipper area. By the time I finally pulled that baby off my pants, there was quite a bit of ventilation added to my new jeans. But, hey, those kinds of issues do not trouble the mind of a kindergarten boy! My grandparents never noticed, so I went off to school that afternoon in my threadbare pants.

After school, I came home, went up to my room to change before dinner, and threw the jeans in the trash. They weren't any good to me anymore with that big hole in them.

My Mom noticed the pants in the trashcan and asked me about them at the dinner table.

"I threw them out," I responded matter-of-factly. "There is a hole in them."

"You don't throw out perfectly good clothes, especially those! They aren't just hand-me-downs from your brothers; they are practically brand new!"

Then the jeans were unearthed from the trash and held up for all to see. My mom was shocked.

"Joshua," she exclaimed, "this is no small hole! The whole inseam of your pants is gone! You wore these jeans to school with that huge hole in the crotch?"

"Yeah, but it was no big deal," I told her nonchalantly. "We didn't do much running around today. It actually was good and made it easier, because we just sat in a circle Indian-style listening to some stories."

My poor mother was mortified and probably glad that we moved to another town a month later. The story has never been deleted from the annals of Finley Family History; in fact, I think it's in the "Classics" section.

A string is a small thing, but in the right location of a pair of jeans, it's critical to the usefulness and life of the pants. Small things have incredibly powerful effects in our life, whether positive or negative.

Most of us have heard the phrase, "Don't sweat the small stuff." Let me be clear: forget and ignore that line of thinking. When it comes to temptation, each of us have deceptively small areas of compromise that have the potential of bringing about major loss in our families, our marriages, our influence, and especially our relationship with the Lord.

Deceptively small things have the potential to bring incredibly big results. Minuscule termites can eat away the wood foundation that supports the structure of your home. One small thread in the hands of a kindergartener can destroy a pair of jeans and yield a lifetime of good-natured embarrassment. Locusts can devour a farmer's entire livelihood, and the little cicadas can set a whole forest's growth back severely. So, sweat the small stuff? You bet! Each of us face daily temptations to compromise, temptations which may appear to be "small" but have a big potential to deceive us and damage our relationship with the Lord, the most valuable relationship we have.

One of the neatest little books in the Bible is the Song of Solomon. King David's son, Solomon, authored it early on in his reign over Israel. The Bible says that Solomon was the wisest man that ever lived (besides Jesus, of course). He wrote over 1,000 songs over the course of his lifetime, but this one was called "The Song of Songs." In fact, more Bible commentaries have been written about this passage than almost any other. Boil down all of the symbolism and truth about love, sex and marriage found in this book, and what you have is a thematic piece of literature on the topic of intimacy.

The Jewish people loved this song and viewed themselves as "married to Jehovah," the one true God, so they made it a tradition to sing it on the eighth day of their Passover feast each year. They looked at their relationship as more than a religion but as a spiritual joining to God.

Today, the book helps us—as modern-day Christ-followers—to look at our love relationship with the Lord, the intimate relationship between Christ (the Groom) and His Church (the Bride). As we read this, men have to learn to get comfortable being called the "Bride of Christ" in the same way that women have to learn to be comfortable being called the "sons of God."

In the passage below, King Solomon has recruited some guys to care for his vineyards. It seems that this group of brothers somehow draw in their sister to help them one day, and as Solomon is checking up on their work, he notices the sister working in his vineyard and a relationship is born. Then comes this powerful statement:

> Song of Solomon 2:15
> *"Catch for us the foxes, the little foxes that ruin the vineyards,*
> *our vineyards that are in bloom."*

This passage in Song of Solomon has so many applications for our lives. The vine easily represents our lives and our connection with God (see John 15). Then there were the sly, fifteen-inch foxes in Palestine that drove the keepers crazy. They would attack the vineyards, biting at the vines and eating the fruit. Like an owner tormented by those pesky little foxes, each of us have small areas of life—sometimes deceptively small areas—that try to damage our relationship to the Lord. They surface with the sole intent to destroy our intimacy with Christ and ruin the fruit of love, joy, and peace that blooms and flourishes out of that connection to Him.

In my opinion, there are five important keys to help protect your relationship with the Lord.

TO PROTECT YOUR RELATIONSHIP WITH JESUS

Key # 1: Respond to God's Call to Greater Levels of Purity

The Bible says that you are God's field. The Psalmist wrote in Psalm 1 that when you meditate on the Word of God you become like a tree planted by streams of water. Jesus said, "I am the Vine." He is our Life source and we're called to bear fruit. As Paul said in Galatians, the Holy Spirit working in our lives produces the fruit of love, joy, peace, and more.

We may not have literal foxes that we tolerate in our gardens, but we all have thought patterns that we grow easily accustomed to and don't exert the energy necessary to drive them out. Now, if they were full-grown wolves, we would take aggressive action to get rid of them. But it's the "little fox thoughts" that we often tolerate as "no big deal"—for a moment here and a moment there—until we have given them so much space that the "vine" of our spiritual life is being ruined and the fruit lost.

There was a casino near where I grew up which had the logo of a fox under a tree. In Native American lore, the fox was cunning and wise, a deceiving trickster, so it would make sense that this casino had a logo that symbolically stated, "You've just been deceived!" All customers coming to the resort with a hope to win their dream, would drive in and walk by a logo that declared in its mocking essence, "We gotcha!" In life, we have similar "little things" that aren't full-blown, blatant sins, but they trip us up. If we let those thoughts fester, the fox says, "Gotcha!"

WHAT ARE SOME OF THE LITTLE FOXES?
Doubt
You and I might say, "I am a believer," but how many of us ever wrestle with the little fox of doubt? When we face something challenging, we may even say things like, "If I just had more faith!" But do we really? Jesus said, "If you only had the faith the size of a mustard seed, you will say to this mountain, 'Move from here to there,' and it will move." The issue is not that we need more faith—because you already have faith; the issue is that we need less doubt. Friend, don't be afraid to bring your doubts to God. Talk about them, don't hide them. God can deal with your doubts better than most people. You don't have to act like you have everything figured out to follow Jesus. He'd rather you bring what's in you than what you think should be in you.

> "We must lay before Him what is in us,
> not what ought to be in us."
> **C.S. Lewis**

Anxiety
I'm one of those people who would fall into the class of humanity called "list makers." I'm always looking at lists of things to do. The only problem is that the list never gets emptied; it's always being added to. Maybe you, like

me, often find yourself running around like Martha in the New Testament—making sandwiches that Jesus never ordered[1], doing lots of good things but never having the feeling that you are well enough prepared or that what you will end up with will be enough. All of this when, like the story in the Bible, Jesus just wants to be with us.

> "Look ahead, don't try to live ahead.
> Looking ahead produces vision, trying to
> live ahead creates anxiety."
>
> ## Joshua Finley

It is so easy to look ahead and start to live emotionally beyond this moment in time, allowing anxiety to creep in. Any time you go through a major change this dynamic tension can intensify, but anxiety is a little fox. It can attack the vineyard anytime, trying to steal your sleep, killing your appetite, and eating the fruit of peace. The bottom line for this fox will always be to damage your connection with the Lord and rob your fruit.

Careless Wounding Words

I'm not a person who swears or abuses my wife, but there are words that come out sometimes that are less than careful. No one would consider them abusive towards Anna or my children. They could even earn some laughs on a TV sitcom. They can seem so little, but once they come out of my mouth, I immediately feel like something is gone from the relationship. Do you ever use these kinds of words? These are the kinds you feel like you need to follow up with, "I was just kidding," or "I didn't really mean it." Down deep, though, you know that a fox has just eaten up some of the fruit of love and kindness in your life, damaged a relationship, and, along with it, your influence.

Greed

I can pretty much guarantee that you are not going to wake up one day, hear a temptation from the enemy like, "Go rob a bank," and then go and rob a bank. The temptation for greed is rarely that overt. But I think of Achan in the Old Testament and how his life was lost due to greed, a level of greed that had been tolerated and cultivated in his heart for a long time. At an opportune time, after the victory over Jericho, he listened to this "little fox" and took a reward for himself from what was ordained to be in the Lord's treasury. The enemy used that greed to bring pain to the nation and destruction to Achan's entire family.

Lust

As long as there is breath in these bodies of ours, we are going to experience little foxes of temptation trying to trap us in impurity and hinder our relationship with the Lord. Lust, simply defined, is a strong desire. I've noticed that sometimes the desire is reaching out from within me to grab something my flesh wants. Other times, because we live in a fallen world with the tentacles of sin all around us, things try to reach in from the outside, seeking to feed the desires within. Either way, they are foxes from the very culture we live in, trying to bite the vines and kill fruit that is maturing in our lives.

When I was in high school I remember thinking, *Why am I having such a hard time curbing a lust for girls?* A certain level of strong desire for the opposite sex is natural and healthy, but what I was dealing with was an area of temptation that deserved to be confronted rather than avoided, even if I wasn't having sex. I knew that the little foxes, those thoughts, had to be dealt with or they wouldn't stay little forever. Those thoughts could have grown into a desire to look at pornography. The internet was becoming more popular at that time, and I thank God that my father decided not to have the internet installed in our house in an effort to protect us. He understood that our self-control at that age was probably not enough to keep us pure.

One of the things I felt that the Lord showed me early on was that my music choices were feeding lustful thoughts and that I needed to make a change. I threw out some music that I had dwelt on. I began to starve those desires and discovered increasing levels of victory. Sometimes you need to adjust your surroundings and monitor what you take in. Your relational connection to Jesus Christ is worth screening out the "little foxes," things like an entertainment choice that can send your mind down a harmful path. I even feel like I have to screen out some of the commercials during an NFL football game for my boys and me, but it's worth it to starve this little fox.

Are there certain people prone to share gossip with you? How can you create a separation? Can you create it through an honest conversation, or will it require steps to spend less time together? Identify and catch those little foxes so that you can guard your relationship with the Lord and the fruit of the Holy Spirit in your life.

DAMAGE DONE. NOW WHAT?

When a small fox has attacked your relationship with the Lord, the natural emotional reaction is a cycle of guilt, discouragement, and condemnation. We may take our disappointment out on others around us and start damaging relationships. It's tough when losing to a little fox not only hurts me but causes others pain as well.

Think about this sequence: your relationship with the Lord has been damaged, resulting in a break in the flow of grace and strength needed for the next temptation. Now you we are feeling even weaker, and you are faced with another temptation: *the temptation to not even try to rebuild.*

Can I encourage you with one word? *Rebuild!* Go ahead, do it. Build again! God is waiting to restore you right away. No need for hooking yourself up to the "kicking-machine" to make sure that you have grieved enough over your poor choice. No need to rehearse a speech, just run home to the Father.

> "Religion: 'I messed up; my Dad is going to kill me.'
> Sonship: 'I messed up; I need to call my Dad.'"
> **Anonymous**

Hear this: whether your "vine" has been bitten by a fox you allowed to thrive, or if you have responded to that failure by provoking further pain—rebuilding and repairing damaged things is almost never easy but is always worth it! The damage to your credibility, to your health, to your credit—sometimes it can look so severe that the thought of rebuilding can be daunting.

When I was a junior in high school, I had a major personal goal in mind. I'm sorry to say that my goal was not to change the entire world. At that point, I just wanted to be cool and bench-press 300 pounds. I was sure I was going to get there. I came closer and closer to the goal, until the day I seriously separated my shoulder diving into second base in a baseball game. Okay, so I wasn't going to be bench-pressing 300 pounds anytime soon. I could accept that—at least temporarily. Then this new height of discouragement came along: the day I found myself in the training room lying on a table while bench pressing a broomstick just to get some level of mobility. *This is going to take me forever,* I recall thinking. *I'll never be able to repair or rebuild this area of my life!* It took a few months, but little by little, as I took care of myself and got healthy, my strength returned to where I was before the injury. What has been lost can be recovered, repaired and repaid. With God as your Source you are never a helpless victim.

I recently heard about an interesting little weasel-like animal found in the Northern Hemisphere called an ermine, or sometimes called a stoat. It's a small, carnivorous critter whose fur turns from brown to a gorgeous soft white in winter. The fur is famous for adorning the historic robes and necks of royalty in Europe. One of the European legends of this species is that the animal would rather die than get their white fur dirty. The hunting strategy was to put a small patch of filthy tar outside the opening of their home, turn the hunting dogs loose to sniff out a trail and get one running, and then chase them down. The theory remains that an ermine would rather give up their life to hunters than return safely to their burrow having had their pure, white coat dirtied by the tar. For this reason, the beautiful ermine has become a symbol of purity.

Jesus also made it clear in the New Testament that purity is a life or death issue. He said that if your eye causes you to sin then gouge it out, and if your hand causes you to sin go ahead and lop it off (see Matthew 5:29–30). He wasn't advocating self-harm. Jesus was emphasizing that there is time for getting so sick of small compromise and the small foxes eating away at the fruit in our lives, that we are willing to humbly present ourselves to the Lord and deal aggressively with the issues at hand. In that place, great transformation is going to happen.

Whatever fox has been eating away at the vineyard of your life or connection to the Lord and whatever fox is trying to eat your fruit of the Holy Spirit, know that without an aggressive, intentional resistance, you are allowing them to steal from you. Continue in the status quo and you will continue to live as a person missing out on the fruit of love, joy, peace, and gentleness.

So, the first key to protecting your relationship with the Lord is to respond to God's call to greater levels of purity. Purity is worth the fight. Let's be like David in the Bible and pray, "Holy Spirit, help; search me and try me. Do a holy audit of my life. Keep me from willful sin. Keep me from foxes that I thought were little but end up doing great damage to my life." (See Psalm 139:23–24) A fresh grace will open up to us, which leads to our second key.

TO PROTECT YOUR RELATIONSHIP WITH JESUS

Key #2: Receive God's Enabling Grace for Greater Levels of Victory

You and I cannot do this in your own strength. A commonly used definition of God's grace is "unmerited favor." That's true, but grace is much more than that! The grace of God is also His divine enablement to do what is humanly impossible. It wasn't just that Christ's righteousness was credited to our spiritual account when we put our faith in Him; He has empowered and strengthened us to LIVE righteously.

So, how will this grace help me to catch and get rid of the foxes? Let's read what Paul says to Titus, his son in the faith, about living in this culture.

Titus 2:11–14 (NIV)
For the grace of God that brings salvation has appeared to all men. It teaches us to say "No" to ungodliness and worldly passions, and to live self-controlled, upright and godly lives in this present age, while we wait for the blessed hope—the glorious appearing of our great God and Savior,

Jesus Christ, who gave himself for us to redeem us from all wickedness and to purify for himself a people that are his very own, eager to do what is good.

The grace of God is more powerful than any little fox, area of compromise, or temptation. When you pray like David, "Lord, search me and try me," and say, "I'm not settling for this in my life anymore," the Holy Spirit will begin to guide you in choices that will help you defeat that thing.

There is an accomplished actor and director by the name of Charles Dutton. You wouldn't have predicted his success by his early years. A middle school dropout, boxer, and a young man who was known not for starting fights but for finishing them, landed in prison for manslaughter. Shortly after that, he had even more years added to his punishment for crimes committed in confinement. Few had any hope for him, thinking he'd either be killed in prison or spend the rest of his life there. But wising up as the years in prison went by, Charles realized that if he survived his term, there was a better way. He later said in an interview, "I adapted to prison life, but I wasn't conditioned by it. I never decorated my cell."[2] Some guys accepted that prison was their lot in life, but Charles Dutton refused to be a prisoner of his past.

Whatever temptation you face, if you've been bound by a certain sin and constantly battling a little fox that just won't go away, don't give up. Whether it has been months, years, decades, or generations of iniquities passed down, you are NOT a prisoner of your past. The grace, or the divine enablement of God Himself, is available to you, to help you say "NO." That grace is stronger than any temptation or fox we will ever face.

Don't identify yourself as a prisoner of sin and start decorating the cell. God's will is to bring you out of that place. Maybe the same small fox of anxiety or gossip or greed or lust has been attacking your life's vines for years. Did you conclude that you are going to have to live with this area of brokenness for the rest of your life? That's not a lie to agree with! Friend, please don't decorate the cell! The Bible says that a righteous man or woman stumbles seven times and the Lord upholds him.[3] That number seven doesn't mean you will be defeated on number eight. It's an expression stating that God has an innumerable number of new beginnings for you. Receive a fresh sense of God's grace from His Word and the promise of His Spirit.

God gave me a revelation one day while I was taking out the trash. I realized that my agreement with the trash company is simply to take what I decide is "trash" to the end of my driveway, then the company is responsible to take it away.

The Lord spoke to my heart that I only needed to listen to Him, accept His definition of what is "trash," and bring Him the trash of my life (sin); He would take care of the rest. He will always cast the sin as far as the east is from the west (see Psalm 103:12). Our job is to bring the garbage to Him, and His promise is to take it away.

It is not always easy to get rid of the little pesky foxes, the areas of weakness in our lives. There was a period of time when Anna and I were continually having a problem with mice taking up residence in our home. As the autumn air turned cold, those critters wanted to move from the surrounding cornfields into our warm Western New York home. We discovered evidence that they were feeding off bits of food in our trashcan underneath the kitchen sink. I recalled a phrase my mentor had many times before—"What you feed will live and what you starve will die"—and we developed strategies accordingly. We tried moving the trashcan outside at night. We got traps to catch those that were inside without catching our own little boys' curious fingers in the process. Unfortunately, the vermin just kept showing up in increasing numbers. It felt like playing one of those carnival games where those critters pop up and you are supposed to whack them on the head, but they just keep popping back up. Sometimes dealing with little foxes and temptations, habits, mindsets, and challenges in our lives can be like that, but stay the course no matter what keeps getting thrown back.

Newlywed friends of ours found themselves challenged with a persistent problem, one the bride had carried into her adult life from childhood. While growing up as a little girl and through her teens, her faraway grandmother consistently mailed her newspaper clippings and articles of girls being kidnapped or raped, beaten or killed. As hard as it is to believe, the grandmother's motive was to communicate care and caution to her granddaughter. The result of this onslaught of horrible news year after year, however, was that this girl grew up having nightmares of being chased or attacked. Despite coming to Christ and growing as a disciple, this young woman was tormented by this pattern of night terrors.

A couple of months into the marriage, the husband decided that the little foxes of fear had to go! Every night before bed, he took his wife's hand and prayed for her against a spirit of fear and against the demonic nightmares. Guess what happened? Well, for a couple of weeks the nightmares actually got worse! Refusing to quit, the prayer battle continued. A couple more weeks in, the new bride began having a few peaceful nights of sleep. The nightmares gradually decreased to one or two a week. Staying on the chase, the nightly prayers continued until the terrifying dreams became rare and then ceased altogether. Then one night as my friend was about to pray once again for his wife's sleep, the Holy Spirit spoke to his heart, "You don't have to pray anymore; just give praise for the victory."

Sometimes when you make the decision to do something about the trash in your life, all hell breaks loose against you—temptations increase, attacks increase, you fall more, and the enemy tries to convince you that it's just never going to work. Stay the course. Avail yourself of His great grace at every opportunity, and eventually those things will weaken. Eventually that fox, that area of temptation, will lose its power. Even Jesus Himself may have been hungry and tired after fasting forty days in the wilderness, but the reason the devil finally left Jesus was because of His consistent resistance.

TO PROTECT YOUR RELATIONSHIP WITH JESUS

Key # 3: Ask God for a Greater Fear of the Lord

> Psalms 25:14 (NKJV)
> *The secret of the Lord is with those who fear Him, and He will show them His covenant.*

Don't we long for a level of relationship with the Lord that's deep enough that He shares His secrets with us? He will do that for "those who fear Him." What does that mean?

> Proverbs 8:13 (NKJV)
> *The fear of the Lord is to hate evil.*

There are some foods I love with a capital "L." You don't have to tie a rope around me and drag me to the nearest Brazilian steakhouse! If I'm not otherwise occupied and you invite me for a good ribeye steak, garlic mashed potatoes, asparagus, and ice cream for dessert, I will RUN there with you. You won't have to sit across from me and prompt me to keep taking bites of my food. If I'm there and it's in front of me, I'm eating it with great enthusiasm! On the other hand, there are some foods I hate, with a capital "H." If I were fasting for a week and was suddenly overcome with hunger, and the only thing to eat in my refrigerator or kitchen was some soft, chewy, gag-me tofu—I'd rather starve to death! You couldn't make me eat it!

The fear of God's judgment will only keep you for a short time. A love relationship with God will keep you for a lifetime.

We have to be honest about the things our flesh loves and those things our flesh hates. We have no problem finding time and reasons to do the things we love, and we have no problem avoiding the things we hate.

Have you ever "hated yourself" for blowing it in the same area of sin, over and over? That's not what God wants! God loves you, and God hates sin. Satan deceives us. He tries to get us to hate ourselves and never acknowledge that our flesh actually LOVES the sin! That's why you do it, because your flesh loves it.

Think about what happens to our thoughts and mood after the moments when we blow it. We wallow in shame for a while before steeling ourselves up again to try to defeat the temptation we know leads to some area of sin or failure. We hate the sin, or so we think. Is it possible that there is a great deception going on here?

The "fear of God" is a powerful key, but usually people misunderstand what it really is. Typically, people think of it as "the fear of God's judgment." While that is a facet of it, the fear of God's judgment will only keep you for a short time. A love relationship with God will keep you for a lifetime.

The Bible says that the fear of God is to hate sin. How can I grow in it? And how does it help me protect my relationship with the Lord and keep me from sin? Of course as believers we hate the sin in our hearts, but we can make great progress if we go before the Lord in prayer and admit, "Father, I thank You that You love me unconditionally. Your love strengthens me. I must admit, however, that my flesh loves this behavior; that's why I get tempted. But I'm asking You to overwhelm me with Your hatred for it."

Now, that kind of faith in God, honesty about ourselves, and appeal towards Heaven can produce a holiness in our lives and a depth of relationship with Him, rather than a weakening of it. That kind of candid approach with God will cause Him to say, "I can trust My secrets to this one."

TO PROTECT YOUR RELATIONSHIP WITH JESUS

Key #4: Respond to the Invitation to Greater Levels of Intimacy.

Everything in this chapter must point to this. As I was reading verse Song of Solomon 2:15 about the little foxes and why it's so important to "sweat the small stuff," my eyes were suddenly drawn back one verse to notice a profound progression in this passage.

> Song of Solomon 2:14 (NIV)
> *My dove in the clefts of the rock, in the hiding places on the mountainside, show me your face, let me hear your voice; for your voice is sweet, and your face is lovely.*

We must never forget that intimacy is offered to us before our purity is ever perfected. This invitation to intimacy was given before the call to greater purity in verse 15. Before Solomon said anything about the little foxes, he said, "Come to me! You are gorgeous!" Before the Lord challenges us about sweating the small stuff, He says, "Come to Me. Let me see your face. You are the apple of My eye. Let Me hear your voice. Don't think you can't pray and talk to Me because you still have issues. No way!" The longer we stay away from God, in fact, the longer we will hold onto our issues.

Solomon, as a natural man, knew that the woman he was getting was not going to be perfect. God also knew what He was getting into with us long before He gave His Son for us and purchased us. He already knew our condition, and yet He longed for and still longs for greater intimacy with us.

I can confidently say that as long as we think we must get our act together before we pursue real intimacy with God, it will never happen. The reason is that without walking intimately with Him, spending time talking to Him, worshiping Him in private, drawing strength and grace from His word and presence, we don't stand a chance in catching the foxes that threaten our lives.

Someone once said that the word "intimacy" equals "into me you see." That is why I don't have a problem sharing Finley "hole in the pant seam" stories with you. We have to see into each other's lives to have relationship. Especially with today's culture and up-and-coming generations, authenticity is the new currency. When you are intimate with God, you can say, "God, this is my life and here are my issues. I need fresh grace. I want to walk with You." We can't sweat the small stuff in our own strength. We can't do it, but with Him, we can.

A MERCIFUL FATHER

Our perspective of our heavenly Father may need some adjustment to help us along this journey. I remember at eleven years old sneaking out of the house one night after dinner when I was supposed to be doing chores and homework. It was a school night, but I had arranged to meet some of my friends whom I had known would be up the street playing. Dad was working late.

I was sure I could successfully get out of the house and play with my friends and then sneak back in unnoticed.

I had only just made it to the end of my street and met up with my friends when, guess who just happened to be rolling up to the stop sign at the end of our road? I tried to pretend like I didn't see his car, but I knew I was dead when I got home. As I ran home, I found myself gripped with fear about the trouble that I was in. I remember standing on the wooden step in the garage that went from the garage to our house for what seemed like an eternity. I stood there picturing the scene about to unfold and speculating. In my mind, I could see my dad sitting in his chair thinking of ways to punish me for my deceitful and disobedient behavior. I thought of several different possible repercussions. For a moment, I would get the courage to grab the doorknob, but then, in fear, I couldn't open the door and would let go of the knob. I stood there on that wooden step outside the door trembling, grabbing the doorknob but then letting go for almost forty-five minutes. Finally, I couldn't take it anymore and opened the door and went in to face my dad.

"Well, you've been standing there awhile," my dad said. "I heard the back step creaking and the door knob for the past forty-five minutes! What kept you out there so long?"

I confessed to him that I was afraid of his reaction, but my worst fears were never realized.

Smiling, he said, "Haven't you tortured yourself enough waiting out there? I'll tell you what: why don't you come up with what you think is a reasonable punishment?" The relief I felt! "What?" I exclaimed. Talk about mercy!

How many times do we do the same thing? We blow it, and in the recesses, or even in the forefront of our minds, we picture our Heavenly Father sitting on His Throne. We're so afraid to approach Him because we don't have every-thing together. But when we make the leap, take the risk, and draw near to Him, we discover that He loves us and has far more grace for us than we could ever imagine. It's worth being reminded: God offers intimacy to us before our purity is ever perfected.

What is the fox that God is helping you identify right now? By His grace, catch and begin removing it from your life. When we, by God's divine enablement, "sweat the small stuff" and catch those little foxes, we discover greater levels of purity, victory, and intimacy.

Perhaps the issue may seem small. Others might say, "What's the big deal?" Don't worry about them. Not everyone's foxes are the same. I can't live out someone else's personal convictions; but I also can't ignore my own. They all have foxes they are fighting too. Surrender it to the Lord as you receive a fresh revelation of His victory and grace upon your life. Overcoming involves sweating the small stuff and reminding yourself He is ready to help you. Because of Jesus' sacrifice, you and I actually live under the smile of heaven.

"A spiritual stronghold is a mindset impregnated with hopelessness that causes me to accept as unchangeable a situation that I know is contrary to the will of God."

MICHAEL CAVANAUGH

03

THE SLIPPERY SLOPE

At eight years old, my parents took me to some friends' house for dinner. When you're from a family with six kids, only certain folks will have you over. Fortunately, this family had a lot of kids, one of which was a boy about my age named Jeremy. They had a lot of land and woods, and, most exciting for me and my friend, was that they had their own pond. Ponds and boys just go together. I just wanted to eat dinner as quickly as possible and get out to the pond, look for frogs, catch some tadpoles, and get as close to the water as we could.

There we were, having a glorious time on a beautiful day. We were down by the water trying to get some tadpoles when, all of a sudden, one of us got stung by a yellow jacket. Unbeknownst to us, we had stepped onto the surface of an underground yellow jacket nest, and pretty soon, both of us were being stung repeatedly.

We immediately began to struggle up the hill. The problem was that we had slid down the muddy embankment to get to the water, and now we were having to get back up the hill quickly to escape the stinging bees. The bank was wet and slippery, difficult to get footing on. Our little scrambling feet were aggravating the nest even more. Yellow jackets were flying up our baggy jeans (no skinny jeans back then), all the while we kept climbing, sliding back down into the nest, and slapping our pant legs as we tried to escape the slope. By the time we made it back to the house, we each had been stung at least twenty-five times. Sin can work that way. It will often entice us downhill looking for one thing but end up stinging us severely.

> "Many of us have up-hill dreams with down-hill habits."
> **John Maxwell**

SIN'S BEGINNING

God created some things and made some things. For example, He created light by speaking it into existence. He created the heavens and the earth. As for trees, He said, "Let the earth bring forth the grass, the herbs, the trees." In effect, the trees come out of the ground, are sustained by the ground, and return to the ground.

God made us (our spirits) from Himself, to be sustained by Him and to return to Him. My body, on the other hand, was made from the dust and is sustained by things that come from the dust (like spinach, broccoli, mashed potatoes, burgers cooked just right on the grill, and ice cream), and then my body goes right back to the dust at the end of life.

What would happen if a plant pulled itself out of the very stuff it was made from? It would be crazy for a plant to say, "I'm done! I'm pulling out of the ground and striking out on my own." It would die after unearthing itself from the very soil that sustains it.

We are made from "God Kind of Stuff." Why do we think it would be any different to pull out of the stuff that sustains us? Adam and Eve were made in the image of God, but when they sinned in the Garden, they essentially "pulled out of God." By being apart from Him, striking out from Him on their own, they died. Their bodies were still alive, but their spirits were totally dead. In time, their bodies also died and returned to the ground.

Sin is not just a nature we caught; it is also a crime we each committed.

To be apart from faith in Jesus Christ then is to be spiritually dead forever and alive in body only. To be in Christ by faith is to be spiritually alive forever.

Sin is not just a nature we caught, but also a crime we each committed. In regard to sin, we have both inherited Adam and Eve's sinful nature and been guilty of the act of commission. As part of the human race, we have the sinful nature in our spirits, making us spiritually dead while physically alive. The Bible is also very clear that all of us have sinned (committed the acts) and fallen short of God's glorious standard and desire for us.

Part of overcoming involves knowing at the core of my being that sin is awful. Sin is awful, and far more destructive than I can even imagine. Grace is awesome. Grace is more powerful than sin, but to apply it effectively, we have to first view sin appropriately. What does sin look like, and how is it like a slippery slope?

THE SLIPPERY SLOPE OF SIN

Sin has some similarity to a bodily infection. My grandfather once had a mouth sore that he ignored for a while, not knowing that he had a tooth infection. It went from his mouth to his heart through his bloodstream and almost killed him!

In the same way that a cut to the human body gets infected if left untreated, sin left unchecked gets worse and becomes a bigger problem. Allowed to grow, sin becomes something that you absolutely don't want to live with! All sin separates us from God and leads to death, but left to grow out of control, it can wreak havoc on a person's life—believer and unbeliever alike.

Sin doesn't discriminate, it just hates! What starts out small can become big, so what begins with one step down a muddy embankment can proceed on a slippery slope to disaster. This is why man's greatest challenge is to know our need for a Savior, for Jesus. We need a Savior to "overcome" our sin.

In the prayer of Psalm 19, David gave some powerful insight into this slippery slope[4].

> Psalms 19:12-14 (NKJV)
> *Who can understand his errors?*
> *Cleanse me from secret faults.*
> *Keep back Your servant also from presumptuous sins;*
> *Let them not have dominion over me.*
> *Then I shall be blameless,*
> *And I shall be innocent of great transgression.*
> *Let the words of my mouth and the meditation of my heart*
> *Be acceptable in Your sight,*
> *O Lord, my strength and my Redeemer.*

David spoke of errors, secret faults, presumptuous sins, sins that bring dominion over you, and the great transgression. None of these are good, but some are stronger than others. They indicate how the steps down this muddy slide can bring your life down to destruction. I want to make some distinctions about these levels, because no matter how you've opened yourself up to these kinds of sin, you can overcome every one of these through the grace of Jesus Christ.

Level 1: Errors

Who can understand his errors?

Errors are like the "smaller" mistakes and infractions that are often born out of ignorance and may not be deliberate steps out of God's will at all. Perhaps a person has just been saved a short time and is not yet familiar with

God's Word. Old lifestyle choices and habits may still be strongly influencing behavior. Four-letter words may still be born out of habit. Entertainment choices may still be born out of past tastes for what is enjoyable. You may be speeding down the highway not even knowing the speed limit changed. Errors are not the highest level of sin. There may be new couples who come to church who are living together, sleeping together, and get saved, who take a while to work through issues. Until the mirror of God's Word is held up, they don't even realize what is right or wrong. When they do see it, they will often say to one another and to me, "Hey, we want to get this right! We want to get married." If you don't yet know God's Word, then you really don't know how to live right.

A common saying in church culture is "Come as you are," and we mean it because you are welcome to come to church, come to Jesus Christ in whatever state of being you might be in. We mean it in terms of what you wear, and we mean it in terms of whatever spiritual state you may be in, what you may believe, and whatever your lifestyle choices may be. We also believe that none of us will stay "as we are" for long as we experience the power, the truth, and the presence of Jesus Christ in our life.

"People who were nothing like Jesus liked Jesus."
Andy Stanley

Jesus was a friend of sinners and we want to be friends of sinners also. We work with new Christians all the time, because grace is more powerful than any sin. Sometimes you and I can only observe what a person is doing, but we need to be careful about making a conclusion about that person's heart based on those observations. We may not know what this behavior was borne out of or what level down the slippery slope their heart resides.

The word "sin" literally means, "to miss the mark." It's an archery term referring to that moment when you pull back and aim for the bullseye—the center being God's absolute best and sin being anything that deviates from that.

"Who can understand his errors?"

You say, "We ALL have sin at the error level!" and you are right. We all have errors. The amazing thing is that God still chooses to use people who make sinful errors. The answer to "Why does God choose people who make sinful errors?" is really quite simple: there are no other kinds of people around! If He didn't use people who fail, He wouldn't have anyone to choose from.

Sin at this "error" level can usually be dealt with on your own if you really are willing to change, through confessing it to God. Of course, the "if you really are willing to change" is key here.

We have seen the Charlie Brown cartoons where he and Lucy are playing with a football. Lucy takes the ball and holds it in place for Charlie Brown to kick. Charlie comes running up as fast as he can and then, just as he reaches the point of no return and expends all of his energy to kick the football, she pulls it back and lifts it up. Poor Charlie Brown! He kicks with all his might, but there's no ball. We watch agonizingly as our beloved Charlie flies into the air and stares at the sky in bewildered shock as his body flips and then painfully slams onto his backside. Lucy does this time and time and time again until Charlie can no longer trust her. Eventually Lucy says, "Let's play football again, Charlie Brown," but he replies,

"I'm done with you. Every single time when I get to the point of no return, you pull the football away and I land flat on my back."

This time Lucy responds tearfully, "Charlie Brown, I'm so sorry. I've been terrible to you throughout the years, picking up the football as I have. I've played so many cruel tricks on you, but I've seen the error of my ways. I've seen the look of hurt and terror in your eyes when I've deceived you. I've been wrong, so wrong. Won't you please give this poor, penitent girl another chance?"

Moved by his remorseful friend, Charlie Brown agrees to kick the football once more. Lucy tees it up, Charlie backs up and comes running as fast as he can, releases all of his energy on this new opportunity to kick it a mile. Just as he reaches that point of no return, Lucy snatches the football up, yet again, and sends Charlie flying uncontrollably into the air, terrorized by both the treachery and the inevitable landing on his back again. Charlie's thud on the ground is then followed up by Lucy's final statement,

"Recognizing your faults and actually changing your ways are two different things, Charlie Brown."

You can know something is sin, but if you don't want to change, you won't. It's one thing to recognize your ways, but it's another thing to say, "God, I want to change. By Your grace, change me. I put my will in cooperation with Your grace. Forgive me of this error. I'm moving on from this level of sin." Many times, you can make that transaction just between you and God when sin is at this level.

Level 2: Secret Faults

Cleanse me from secret faults.

There is a level of sin that is not so visible but takes a different approach to root out—the "secret faults." Maybe your spending is out of control and you are hiding it from your spouse. Maybe you are paralyzed with envy or harboring bitterness within. Some married persons find it easy to slip into texting, communicating, and otherwise emotionally connecting with some-one other than their spouse. Young people will send things to each other on social media that are totally inappropriate and the messages will disappear with seemingly no accountability for the young boy or girl. Internet porn is a secret fault for many.

The weight of living a double life with a secret sin is awful. David wrote about this from personal experience. He said that his strength was sapped while he kept his sin a secret; it evaporated out of his body like the morning dew be-cause of the guilt he was carrying. It was weighing down on his soul. Then he declared, "I will confess my sins and regain my strength." Bringing that fault to the light brought new strength back into his being.

Professional counselors have said to me, "We are only as sick as our secrets." The truth is that we can have authority over what we are willing to talk about.

Lance Armstrong, the phenomenal and legendary cyclist, was a man many came to admire for his disciplined training regimen, his determination to whip cancer, and his unparalleled accomplishment of winning the Tour de France seven times. Yet he was carrying a secret, living a double life. The athletic achievements were incredible, but behind the trophies was a man that for thirteen years had successfully hidden a performance-enhancing drug habit. He hid it from the government, from his kids, from all of the regulatory systems in place in the cycling world, and from all of the investigators. Through repeated denials, the vicious attacks of others, threats of lawsuits and any means possible, he fought to keep the secret under wraps. Finally, he could not hide it any longer and spilled the truth in a TV interview. "Yes, I did it," he acknowledged. "I hid it." Then there was this painful but powerful admission: "I lost myself in the process."

When the enemy convinces you that it would be better for you to hide your secret sin than to come out with it, you lose a part of who you are and you struggle silently. It can be an eating disorder, a sexual addiction, overeating, cutting, or closet drinking.

You can usually break the power of sin at this level by confessing to a mature, trusted person or leader and bringing it to the light.

Whatever the secret is, it's always better to come to the light with that secret fault than to try to deal with it yourself. First of all, the devil is the "father of lies." Jesus said that the enemy cannot speak anything else but lies. It's the devil's native language. So, when you hear, "Just keep it to yourself; you can handle it," know that he is lying to you! You cannot handle it. There is this slippery slope of sin you are stepping down into and your enemy knows that isolation feeds delusion.

There are errors and secret faults, and then there are the presumptuous sins.

Level 3: Presumptuous Sins

Keep back Your servant also from presumptuous sins

The next level of sin down the slippery slope is a presumptuous, or deliberate, sin. You know that it's wrong; that's not the issue. The presumption at this level is that "I can sin and ask for forgiveness later." This level of sin is intentional. Have you ever played that game in your mind where you thought, *I know this is wrong, but I know God loves me and will forgive me?* I have more times than I like to remember.

Why is this kind of sin so dangerous? Because this sin will mess with your conscience, and it erodes your will power. The attitude will start to develop that says, "Oh, what the heck? I can get free anyways. God forgives."

Presumptuous sin is a trap! It's a dangerous trap!

A long-time friend of mine told me a story about his grandfather who was diabetic, in failing health, and kind of on the stubborn side. The elderly man actually picked up the phone and dialed 911, to which dispatch answered and asked, "Sir, what are your symptoms?" This grandfather answered, "I don't have any yet, but I am about to eat a pound cake!" The man actually did this *four times* before the family had to intervene and emphasize why he couldn't do it anymore.

Yes, it is true that when we sin God will forgive us. But what we must also realize is that every time we sin intentionally, we are weakening our convictions and conscience, and we are eroding our will power to resist sin in the future.

The Hebrew word for this kind of prideful sin comes from a root word, "zud," which actually means "to seethe" or "boil over."

Cooks have to have an innate ability to do several things at once; I, however, am a very focused, one-dimensional person who would not make a very good chef. Nevertheless, I have tried my best to help Anna on a few occasions with something like potato salad. One time, I had a pan heating on the stove, boiling the potatoes; then I turned over to another counter and began chopping some celery or other vegetables. Suddenly, the potatoes back on the stove started making noise. I had put the heat up too high and ignored it too long. When the potatoes on the stove started to boil, there was a spitting sound of foam and flame hissing at me while the starch overflowed in a noisy mess that could not be hidden.

> **Sin takes you where you don't want to go, keeps you longer than you want to stay, and costs you more than you ever wanted to pay.**

That's exactly what happens to prideful, presumptuous sins. What that Hebrew word indicates is that presumptuous sin, which we insist on keeping private due to pride, will boil over publicly. The sin I believed I could manage and keep secret will lead to being found out in a very public display, the timing of which will not be my choice. At that point, you can no longer pretend that it didn't happen. Everybody knows it happened! It boiled over and made a mess!

How do you deal with sin at this level? There is only one way. Deal with it head on by humbling yourself, owning the mess, cleaning up the mess, making restitution wherever you can, and come to God. You will, however, need help from others. You will have to build an accountability system of support around you that opens the door to rebuild trust. You can't just figure it out on your own and handle it by your own will power, because you have already allowed sin to get to a point that it's becoming uncontrollable. This leads me to the next step down the slippery slope of sin.

Level 4: Sins That Bring Dominion

Keep back Your servant also from presumptuous sins; Let them not have dominion over me.

This level down the slope of sin indicates that the sin you thought would be "cool" and satisfying, the sin "that you could stop when you wanted," now holds you hostage because you can't stop. You can't stop thinking it, doing it, spending it, saying it, going there, or taking it in. The trap that the enemy set for you has a hold on you.

Sin develops an appetite that will never be satisfied by more sin. This trap can be any addiction. What can start out as a recreational drug can take you hostage. This bondage can also apply to pornography, videogaming, gossip, overeating, negative thinking, or even social media. There was even a TV show on addictions called "My Strange Addiction," and there are some unusual ones out there! One review of that show said, "Addictions are fascinating, but too much time is spent gawking at their odd behavior as opposed to treating it." God wants you free of the dominion of sin even more than you do.

Like the boys who went looking for tadpoles but ended up getting stung by a swarm of bees, sin causes you to go looking for one thing but ends up giving you something else. In this case, at the bottom of the slope is a bondage to something entirely different from the pleasure you sought. The old saying is very sobering and true, "Sin takes you where you don't want to go, keeps you longer than you want to stay, and costs you more than you ever wanted to pay."

Why do we sometimes stay in patterns of dominion-level sins when we actually have the power to walk away from them? The answer to that question relates to the idea of strongholds. When thought patterns of ungodly beliefs and lies go unstopped and unchallenged, we are building, brick-by-brick, a fortress, erecting a foothold in our life that the Bible calls a "stronghold." It is something that started as an error, but left unchecked, can become a stronghold.

Michael Cavanaugh, the President of Elim Bible Institute & College, said this: "A spiritual stronghold is a mindset impregnated with hopelessness that causes me to accept as unchangeable a situation that I know is contrary to the will of God."

When a stronghold is established, I am convinced that I'm not hitting the mark. I am also convinced that I will never be able to hit the mark, or the devil convinces me that the mark is in the wrong spot and to aim for something else.

Elephants are amazing animals with excellent long-term memories. There is a technique circus trainers use to train elephants, which helps me understand how the enemy builds a stronghold in our minds. Trainers don't want elephants running through circus tents, damaging property, or using their power to destroy. When a baby elephant is small and not nearly as powerful as it will one day become, trainers bind the elephant with a chain to a stake in the ground in such a way that if the elephant pulls to get away, the chain hurts it. The youngster will try and try to pull free and go where it wants, but because he feels and remembers the pain of pulling, he eventually stops trying to escape.

In time, that elephant grows larger and larger, stronger and stronger. Although the animal is far more powerful than it was before, its vivid memory serves as a detriment. With one swift movement, the grown elephant could easily be set free from its bondage, but its memory of the past keeps it bound in the present. Trainers have learned that the elephant's memory and fear of pain will keep them from attempting to pull away from the small stake that keeps them chained in place. They can use the same stake when the elephant is an adult, and because of the imprint on the elephant's memory, that small stake might as well be a million-pound anchor. The elephant's mind says, "I can never break free from this thing." The elephant's memory of the past has sealed its fate in the future.

Many times, our present and future freedom is sabotaged by our memory of the past. A major part of overcoming is remembering to forget. It's time to get past your past. You have been made a new creation in Christ and that sin shall not have dominion over you!

If you are struggling with dominion-level sin, yes, you need forgiveness. You also need deliverance (freedom) and to avail yourself of every opportunity to replace the ungodly lies with God's truth. The power of those lies and their permission to occupy space in your life needs to be rejected. We have a God who will forgive you AND deliver you.

"I'm a Christian! Deliverance?" Yes, sometimes a Christian needs God's deliverance from dominion-level sins, and that deliverance can come to you in many ways and through many different means. God is not holding this against you. He's saying, "Let me set you free from that!" God's help can come in an instant or it can come by consistently availing yourself of His Presence and grace until that day you look back and realize—you are not in the same prison anymore. (Christians cannot be demon-possessed. Once a person becomes a born-again child of God the Holy Spirit resides in the temple of their body. However, they can certainly be oppressed by demonic influence that is invited in through sin, lies, trauma and generational curses.)

The motivation to get out from under this power of sin can vary. Some just want freedom from this "thing" because they want joy back in their life. Some people want freedom because they don't want to be exposed. Often, people deal with sins that they don't want their kids to struggle with also, because "what doesn't get healed gets handed down." Whatever the motivation is, bring it to the light and let the grace of God come in.

When you ask a trusted leader or mature fellow believer to pray for you, he or she is not going to think less of you; they are going to respect you. In fact, if you really want to be free, you won't care what people think anyway! Deliverance received is more valuable than dignity maintained in the eyes of others.

At this stage on the slippery slope of sin, you cannot proceed forward on your own. You need help from God and from people. That's why I love faith-based recovery groups where hurts, habits, and hang-ups are being lifted off of believers. Our church has Freedom groups which are incredibly transformative. (For more information on Freedom small groups, check out Church of the Highlands.) It's in groups like those where the determination to not allow sin to have dominion motivates you to confess, get support, and let God re-program your thinking. It's there where your mind can align with His truth instead of with what the enemy has been saying to you and about you. I was born to think like man but I've been born again to think like God! There is power in coming to a place where you can confidently declare with others that "we believe in the victorious Christian life Jesus paid for, and we are on our way there together."

Level 5: The Great Transgression

Then I shall be blameless, and I shall be innocent of great transgression.

Transgression is the worst kind of sin in the Bible, so "great transgression" then is the most dangerous. When the slippery slope gets to this level, you know that it's sin, you know that it's bad, but you're not willing to deal with it. You're trapped by it, unwilling to pursue forgiveness or get help in dealing with it out of personal pride. Your heart is hardened, and your conscience is numb.

This is like Pharaoh in Egypt saying, "Whatever!" This is, "I'm going to resist God." This is like the Pharisees living lives that are so focused on the outward appearance of holiness and rule keeping while their hearts were so hardened to the living God that they committed the great transgression. This is, "I am going to surrender my place on the worship team, leave the church, and I'm going to live the way I want without a care about what God or anybody else thinks!"

If you are thinking right now, "Josh, I'm worried. I'm concerned that maybe I committed the unpardonable sin. I'm afraid that I might have committed great transgression," let me assure you: if that is the posture of your heart, then you have not committed the great transgression. A person who is at this level of sin would not care whether or not they had done so. The unforgivable sin is not some particularly awful sin committed by a person before or after accepting Jesus Christ, and it's not that you thought or said something terrible about the Holy Spirit. The only sin that is unforgivable is to deliberately resist the Holy Spirit's invitation to yield to Jesus Christ until death ends your last opportunity.

> "The same sun that melts ice hardens clay."
> **Bill Johnson**

The same sun that melts ice hardens clay. It's the posture of your heart that will determine whether you get to—or stay in—this level of sin. How you respond when God draws you back to Himself and when the Holy Spirit woos you back up the sinful slope determines which way up or down the slope you go. Will you begin to slide towards this area of the great transgression or return to right standing with God?

We have stories in the Bible of people who seemingly lived their entire lives committing the great transgression, and yet they turned their hearts to God near the end and received His gifts of mercy and forgiveness. Manasseh, one of the most wicked kings you could ever read about, lived a textbook case of a hardened heart and a life of great transgressions; however, God turned even his heart back before it was too late.

WHAT NOW?

So, here's the question: How can I overcome my struggle with sin? David followed his mentions of these different levels of sin by saying this:

> *Let the words of my mouth and the meditation of my heart be acceptable in Your sight, O Lord, my strength and my Redeemer.*

That is my prayer and yours as well, and that's where the book *Overcome* is going to go: replacing the lies that yield only counterfeit pleasures with the truth that produces the joy and freedom you were made for. I'll close this chapter with three things to consider.

1. The Humanity and Example of Jesus

Hebrews 4:15
This High Priest of ours understands our weaknesses, for he faced all of the same testings we do, yet he did not sin.

In all of recorded human history, nobody had ever run the mile in under four minutes until England's Roger Bannister did so in 1954. Since he broke that barrier, many have performed the feat; it happens all the time in elite running circles. It seems the mental block of "it's impossible" had to be removed.

Yes, Jesus was God, but as the Son of Man, as a man in right relationship with God, He defeated sin. This encourages me. If nobody else had ever done it, I'd have no hope! Because He lived as a man facing all the same testing we do and was without sin, I am inspired by His example that defeating sin can be done.

2. The Promise of the Holy Spirit and a Way of Escape

> I Corinthians 10:13
> *The temptations in your life are no different from what others experience. And God is faithful. He will not allow the temptation to be more than you can stand. When you are tempted, he will show you a way out so that you can endure.*

One can always predict that characters like McGyver, Jack Bauer, and Raymond Reddington are going to escape the tough spots they find themselves in on TV. We know they will get out of it. With God, there is a promise that we can escape any temptation that comes our way. In fact, the word provision "pro" meaning to proceed or come before and "vision" which comes from the Latin root "vid" where we get our word "video" or to see. When the Bible says that God *provides* a way out, it means that God saw before what you and I needed in that moment of temptation and already provided a way of escape! Jesus is so many steps ahead of our enemy! Before our forefather Adam ever transgressed, the Lamb of God was slain to pay the penalty for our sin.

Not only do we have the example of Jesus, but we have the Promise of the Holy Spirit so that we are not left as orphans. Rather than fearing temptation and any potential fall, feel free to adopt a little smirk. For with the help of the Holy Spirit, you are the "escape artist", "a God-fearing Houdini" who has a path marked out for you by God.

3. Hope in the Reality of Our Newly-Created Identity

2 Corinthians 5:14-17
Since we believe that Christ died for all, we also believe that we have all died to our old life. He died for everyone so that those who receive his new life will no longer live for themselves. Instead, they will live for Christ, who died and was raised for them. So we have stopped evaluating others from a human point of view. At one time, we thought of Christ merely from a human point of view. How differently we know him now! This means that anyone who belongs to Christ has become a new person. The old life is gone; a new life has begun!

You have the example of Jesus, an escape from temptation promised to you, and you are going to experience the reality of the new life Christ gives to you. This is going to be a theme passage for much of this book, because there is power in understanding who you are in Christ, believing it, and owning it.

If you doubt that you can experience such victory over sin, keep looking in the right direction and you can reach your goal. For example, in baseball, the basic goal of every batter is to get safely to first base and then hopefully make it to home plate. There is a trick, though, that every coach teaches: you can never get to first base if, when you're up to bat, you stare at first base while you swing. You have to keep your eye on the ball being pitched to you.

This book is purposed to put tools in your toolbox to beat the problems. What works is NOT focusing on the problem we're trying to beat, but on the Lord Jesus who already beat the problem. Like a batter who gets to the goal (safely to first base) by concentrating on the ball, you'll get to your goal (victory over sin) by keeping your eyes on the ball (loving Jesus Christ).

Philippians 1:6 (NIV)
He who began a good work in you will carry it on to completion until the day of Christ Jesus.

"You cannot build
a powerful life on
a negative focus."

———————————

JOSHUA FINLEY

04

THE REAL PROBLEM WITH PORN

This chapter is for a number of different people: it's for those who are struggling with porn and want help. It's for those wanting to protect and properly train up their children and grandchildren to face this serious issue. It's for those who are not addicted, but have given in to this temptation from time to time. It's for those that are gripped with guilt and condemnation, seeking forgiveness and freedom. And finally, it's also for those who view porn and aren't convinced that it's a damaging sin, or that it's a degrading habit.

I'm not a "finger pointer" or an accuser; I am a man in love with God's people who wants to get in the ring with you and work together to help you win this battle. I want to come into agreement with what the Holy Spirit is saying inside of you and your conscience, as an ally of yours. It's time to overcome. Overcome our thinking related to pornography or any level of addiction. It really is possible.

Possibly the worst quote I've ever heard came from Woody Allen: "Sex without love is an empty experience, but as empty experiences go, it's one of the best." I consider it one of the worst quotes of all time because of how damaging the implications of it are.

I was so proud of my son Jesse, who at only 8 years old, got my attention before dinner one night. He had that look on his face like "I've broken something and I better fess up," but he said, "Dad, I have to talk to you before dinner. I didn't do anything wrong, but something happened that just has me not feeling good inside." He told me that a conversation came up at the school cafeteria that day and one of the boys in his grade began to talk about the things he looks at on the internet at home. That boy hadn't brought anything to school to show my son and his classmates, but was just talking about it with them. I am so grateful for the opportunity to help Jesse process what happened that day. I had already had some conversations about porn with him before, and I'm so glad I did! If it is being discussed at the lunch table in school, we better be discussing it at home and in church.

Pornography is something that can "ambush" people. My first exposure to it was in 5th grade, on a bus on the way home from school. A couple of guys from the nicest neighborhood in our community, boys from good homes, with both sets of parents, brought a magazine on the bus that they must have gotten from someone else in the home. It was my first look at this thing called "porn."

Before going further, I want to differentiate between "innocence" and "purity." Innocence is "being protected from exposure to a particular sin." Purity is "being empowered to make a good choice when faced with a bad option." While I want to keep my children in a state of innocence as long as I can, my ultimate goal is to empower them to make good choices when faced with options.

You cannot build a powerful, pure life on a negative focus. Whatever gets your focus gets you.

Anna laughs at me, probably in a very nervous way, whenever I'm driving, because if I start looking at some site along the way, the car starts to wander towards what it is I'm staring at. Our goal must be to develop a "yes" towards God that is stronger than my "no" towards sin! Focusing on the "no" causes many to wander that way. The determination to say "no" to stuff weakens and wanes over time, but a powerful "yes" to the Lordship of Jesus Christ can grow with unlimited potential.

HOW WIDESPREAD IS THE ISSUE OF PORNOGRAPHY?

Studies vary a little, but indicate that the average child is exposed to pornography between the ages of 9 and 11 years old.

Court systems are taking a stand that I appreciate, stating that sexual abuse of a child can occur without physical touch, because the brain is the most important organ in the human body that responds to sexual stimulation. When an adult shows a child pornography, thankfully the courts are looking at it as abuse, without anyone touching the child, because of the effects this horrific crime has on a child's mind and life.

68% of men in the church regularly view porn or are caught in some form of sexual bondage. Some might argue with those percentages, but I don't care if those numbers are too high or too low. I'm not okay with this level of involvement in the pews!

Interestingly, this issue of porn is not just a problem for guys. When a woman struggles with this, it can carry a weightier load of shame, because it's usually spoken of as a male issue. The woman feels a heavier load of lies bearing down on her soul, feeling like she's a rarity and stands alone among women in the trap of this sin. Girls, I want you to hear me well: while many things said here and in other places about pornography addiction may seem geared towards men, if you are struggling with this issue, in Christ there is forgiveness and freedom for you. You are NOT the only woman on the planet in that place of struggle!

The first porn support group in the US run for women by women was found-ed by Crystal Renaud, who also wrote a new book on women's addiction to porn called *Dirty Girls Come Clean*. A committed Christian, Renaud first came across porn at the age of 11 in a magazine that belonged to her brother. She was addicted for eight years before she got her wake-up call after she arranged an anonymous hook-up with a man she met online.

Renaud recalls: "I had no friends, no passions. I had one mission and purpose in my life: pornography. Any way I could find it, I would. It didn't matter where I was or what I was doing. At home, school, my friend's houses, summer camp and yes, even at church: my addiction came along too."

She continued: "Porn. Masturbation. Cybersex. Webcam sex. Phone sex. Anything you could think up, I watched, experienced and tried to enjoy. No matter how many times I said I would stop, I would just keep doing it."

As a trained counselor, Crystal now calls women's addiction to pornography "widespread and silent." In almost every case, the women she meets believe they are the only ones ever to have struggled with the issue. "Porn and sexual addiction has always been referred to as a man's problem," says Renaud, "but for women it's an unspoken struggle."

Rather than "Shame on you," my mantra is again, "Shame OFF you!"

Porn comes in different levels as well. Even romance novels, often referred to as "Chick Porn," are genre of literature which takes the reader consistently into fantasies about the perfect, most exhilarating romantic encounters, feeding unhealthy expectations and breeding dissatisfaction with real life marriage.

MORAL, THEOLOGICAL, BIOLOGICAL, AND LOGICAL REASONS TO FLEE PORNOGRAPHY

The reason I'm so passionate about this issue is because you can't live with strong convictions if your conscience is screaming at you all the time! Followers of Jesus want to love the Lord with all of their heart, soul, mind and strength. When people get free from this sin, their whole countenance changes. They are more bold, more confident, and exude more life. Porn divides the heart and soul, damages the mind, and steals your strength.

John 10:10 (NKJV)
The thief does not come except to steal, and to kill, and to destroy. I have come that they may have life, and that they may have it more abundantly.

The enemy wants to steal your peace, steal your purity, steal your joy, and rob your sex life of the redemptive potential that Jesus wants you to have.

When it comes to lust, the Bible says "flee!" It doesn't say "stand there and fight it" because it's really difficult to fight something that you are created to flee away from. The only advice or strategy the Bible gives on this subject is "Get away! Flee!"

There are plenty of reasons to do so, and I don't mean just "moral" reasons, although the moral ones are serious. There are physical reasons, and just plain simply logical reasons, for fleeing pornography; even secular sources are recognizing them. It has been said on a recent popular TV talk show that pornography addicts have a more difficult time recovering from their addictions than cocaine addicts, because coke users can get the drug out of their system, but pornographic images stay in the brain forever. "Fightthenewdrug.org" is a grassroots, secular movement that says there are biological and logical reasons for avoidance of pornography as well.

As believers in love with God, we have moral reasons for avoiding porn, but sometimes until you play something out to its logical and devastating conclusion, you don't know why God said this will damage your life. The issue of pornography is more damaging, destructive, and degrading than anyone really wants to consider but we need to for some important reasons.

Here are a few:

1. Porn feeds the demand for the WORST industry ever created in the history of mankind.

Sex slave trafficking and sexual abuse of children are at epidemic levels. There are more slaves in the world today than at any time in human history, and it stems from sex addictions.

There are those who benefit financially from this as very big business. Every click on a computer image or view of a video provides and feeds information to the "degrading menu" of trafficking business makers. What people watch and click on is communicated in such a way so that more of the same can be provided and therefore feed the growing and lucrative addiction, and further enslave people: men, women and children.

"Oh, I'm just looking at an image!" someone says.

No, just follow the image a little further and you are feeding some of the most diabolical living situations that you could imagine.

Porn is basically video prostitution. No man, woman or child grows up with the dream of becoming a porn star, nude poser, or video prostitute. The choice to participate in that lifestyle comes from desperate need and despair. Some have gone on TV doing interviews saying that they only allow themselves to be used this way because they are just paying off college debts. This grieves me, because no matter how you color this business, it's totally corrupt to the root.

2. Porn Creates a Degrading Message

It's a big-time lie being believed, that women are "worthy of love" only if they are worthy of sexual desire! The result is that women are abused, subject to anger and violence, develop eating disorders, and even commit suicide due to the pressures that this industry and addiction create. The average worldwide life expectancy for women is 72 years and 8 months (higher in America), but for a woman caught in the prostitution industry, their lifespan is closer to 50 years old.

3. Porn Creates Sexual Confusion in the Souls of Men and Women

When someone views porn, their intent is not to view members of the same sex but to see people of the opposite sex. The images they get, especially in videos however, include members of both sexes coming together, and so when people are watching and seeing these images, and experiencing "arousal confusion," their soul has trouble sorting out clearly what is arousing them more, men or women.

I had a friend in college who wrestled with pornography and found himself completely mixed up about his own sexual identity. He felt guilt and shame and didn't know if he was gay or heterosexual. Thankfully, he's come through it and now has a beautiful family and shares his testimony of that whole season of his life and God's faithfulness in helping him.

You can't just tell someone, "Don't do it because it's bad." We have to understand this issue of porn comprehensively and see how bad it really is.

4. Porn Wreaks Havoc on the Brain

Back in the 80's there was an interesting 15-second commercial put out by the Partnership for a Drug-Free America. It showed some grease in a frying pan and a voice said soberly, "This is drugs." Then an egg was cracked, opened, and dropped into the hot grease and began frying vigorously. The voice then spoke again, "This is your brain on drugs. Any questions?"

The effect porn has on your brain is staggering. Michael Cusick said this in "Relevant Magazine:"

If some malevolent being held a competition to create the perfect delivery mechanism to enslave our human desire, internet pornography would win the grand prize. Online pornography is fundamentally different from the Playboy or Penthouse of past generations. If the magazines, videos and DVDs of the past were like the Wright Brothers' plane at Kitty Hawk, then internet porn would be a supersonic jet.

Although supersonic jets are impressive for military use or high-speed travel, you wouldn't want one landing in your backyard. But this is the impact internet porn makes on the brain. Its sheer power and intensity create a heightened level of stimulation that your brain was never intended to experience. Because of this, the brain of a person regularly using porn can change and shape itself to resemble neural pathways similar to those of an alcoholic or drug addict.

Doctors are comparing porn to heroin and cocaine addiction because of its strength, but different because of the remaining images on the brain. We know from neural science that your brain can change and heal, and of course we know that God can heal and cleanse and restore, but how severe is this thing called pornography?

DEFINING THE DAMAGE

The "Click ... Drip Affect"

Every time somebody clicks on a pornographic image, there is a dripping of dopamine in the pleasure center, or reward center, of the brain. The pleasure center of the brain gets stimulated by food, by bonding with friends, and by healthy sex. It releases binge mechanisms and cravings for more that, if not coupled with self-control, can cause people to overdose even on things that are good (food for instance).

That pleasure center is getting flooded by dopamine when a person is viewing porn. That's why people will click and click and click and get sucked in for longer and longer periods of time.

Even secular and evolutionary scientists are observing the impact of porn on the brain and the resultant effects on individuals and society and acknowledging that this is negative.

Nudity and Novelty

The longer a person looks at porn, nudity is no longer enough. Novelty becomes important! New kinds of pornography, new images, stronger impulses are needed to satisfy the hunger. The soul searches for an experience that will reproduce that drip of dopamine in the pleasure center. Something as simple as a "soft porn" swimsuit issue, which worked to bring arousal before, won't work again, and it becomes easy to slip into a deeper gutter of depravity.

STRUCTURAL DAMAGE TO THE BRAIN

Excess exposure to the drip of dopamine, through viewing pornography over long periods of time, causes a dulling of the brain's pleasure center. Medical research comparing brain scans of heroin addicts to those of people addicted to pornography find baffling evidence of similar, significant and severe damage being done to the frontal cortex of the brain.

The brain damage effect is real. Pleasured response gets numbed. Persons often enter a "grey world" that seems less colorful, and relationships more shallow. The willpower section of the brain has been eroded so severely that other areas of life are often affected as well, so as a result of the weakened self-discipline, a person spends more, eats more, and gambles or plays video games more.

Italian "Demise of Guys / Resurrection of Guys" Study

Ironically some Italian scientists, from the land known for its romanticism, led the way in a test group of ex-porn addicts. These men didn't stop using porn for moral reasons, but for logical and physical reasons. They stopped because of the trauma of two simple words: "Erectile Dysfunction!"

The Italian Society of Andrology and Sexual Medicine in 2011 released results that were astounding. Dr. Carl Foresta entitled the report "Porn May be Killing Young Men's Sexual Performance." Dr. Forest is quoted:

"Viagra and other erection enhancing drugs don't help with this problem because the problem is not below the belt with blood flow issues. Porn-induced ED arises in the brain … It starts with lower reactions to porn sites. Then there is a general drop in libido, and in the end it becomes impossible to get an erection."

I find it so sad that it takes this extreme symptom to get people's attention about the dangers when there are so many other symptoms along the way, other symptoms that are often ignored until the habit starts to affect the person's sex life.

What other symptoms? All of these other non-ED symptoms are evident in women who view porn, as well as the men: depression, social anxiety, memory impairment, and a loss of motivation in school, college or in employment situations. By not being able to maintain attention span and focus, all of this leads to loss of jobs or dropping out of school.

Porn-Induced ED Recovery Times

How long till a person gets their "mojo" back after quitting pornography for biological or moral reasons? What scientific studies are discovering is astonishing! Older men, 50-years and over, can recover physically in around 2 months. Younger men require at least twice as long! Why? The older guys didn't start on today's internet porn! Peak time for dopamine levels and neural plasticity (moldable part) in the brain is during the teenage years and into your twenties.

The good news of course is that the brain can be healed! Be realistic about that however, because full recovery has to do with a lot more than just the physical restoration. All of those other symptoms need to dissipate also. That level of full recovery for a porn addict usually requires three to five years of sobriety, and with a very strong and intense support system.

The enemy of your soul doesn't give you an accurate scenario at first glance.

He will never give you the picture of porn consequences up front, when you take a quick look at a nude image online. He's never going to tell you "Hey I want you to get on a slippery slope towards brain damage." He's never going to tell you "You are right now feeding the worst, darkest industry affecting humanity in the world!" Nor does he mention "Oh, you think this is about arousal and medicating yourself from stress, but I'm going to ruin your sex life in the process."

Satan comes to steal, kill and destroy you, your family, and your sex life, but God knows that what He has created in reality is better than the "virtual," and He is in the healing and restoration business!

Romans 8:6-7
So letting your sinful nature control your mind leads to death. But letting the Spirit control your mind leads to life and peace.

Romans 12:2
Don't copy the behavior and customs of this world, but let God transform you into a new person by changing the way you think.

HOW DOES A PERSON GET PAST THIS?

1. Admit the Sin

If you have viewed pornography, if it's a habit, if you are viewing it now, or an addict of it, you've got to start here at the place of admission. This process applies for other struggles as well. After David committed adultery with Bathsheba and was found out, he wrote these words:

Psalm 51:1-3 (NIV)
Have mercy on me, O God, according to your unfailing love;
according to your great compassion blot out my transgressions.
Wash away all my iniquity and cleanse me from my sin.
For I know my transgressions, and my sin is always before me.

The issue of keeping your conscience clean is a priority in life, whether it's an individual act of sin (referred to as a "transgression") or a bent or weakness towards particular sin (called an "iniquity"). One thousand people were recently polled with the question: "Would you rather have your entire computer history given to all of your friends and family, or would you rather live right next to an extremely active and volatile volcano?"

Anyone want to guess the outcome of that poll? How would you answer? The vast majority of those polled said they would choose to live next to the volcano; the volcano won by a landslide. They'd rather put their own life in harm's way than have their internet search history exposed.

Former NFL Football player, actor, and TV star Terry Crews, in a Facebook video about his "dirty little secret" of a pornography addiction that gripped him for years, discussed how it messed up his life. He told no one for years, and it got "real bad" in his words. Day turned into night and he was still watching. His wife left him because he had "disconnected" from her. He literally had to go to rehab because it became such a major problem. In a profound and frank discussion of his past, Terry explained the powerful discovery he made:

"By not telling people, it becomes more powerful. But when you tell, and when you put it out there in the open just like I'm doing right now to the whole world, it loses its power."

There are a couple of popular sayings about bad habits that "We are only as sick as our secrets" and "What we hide doesn't get healed." Here's the contrasting and exciting truth, however: when we stop hiding, God starts healing!

2. Agree With God

Psalms 51:4 (NIV)
Against You, You only, have I sinned, And done this evil in Your sight; so You are right in Your verdict, and justified in when You judge.

The word "confession" in the New Testament is not a complicated word; it simply means "I am saying what You are saying!" It means that being in agreement with the Lord about an issue, I declare about my sin what God says about my sin. "My sin is having devastating effects on people I love and other people I've never even met." That's confessing it.

3. Ask for Cleansing and Renewal

> Psalm 51:10-12 (NIV)
> *Create in me a pure heart, O God,*
> *and renew a steadfast spirit within me.*
> *Do not cast me from your presence*
> *or take your Holy Spirit from me.*
> *Restore to me the joy of your salvation*
> *and grant me a willing spirit, to sustain me.*

David's prayer is so powerful, whether you are dealing with pornography, alcohol, or any other addiction. "Renew" and "Restore" are pleas from a heart that is feeling so dull. "The Gray World of Pornography" is dominating, but the person seeks to get into right relationship and into a life of purity. "Grant me a willing spirit" speaks of the dynamic power unleashed when our will-power comes into agreement with God's will, lining up together in a way that His will sustains me.

God cleanses sin, and so it's important to differentiate between temptation and sin, because Satan will lie to you. Temptation is not a sin itself. Sin is sin.

God renews when people are battling either guilt or shame. "Guilt" is that dirty feeling you have because of something you've done. "Shame" on the other hand tries to lie to you and convince you that because of what you've done, you have become something else and are therefore now "less." Shame sticks to you longer than guilt, because while guilt is about what you do, shame is about who you are! The Bible says that on the cross Jesus bore our guilt AND our shame. He wore it! He hung there carrying it and paying the price for it, so that you and I could be made new.

Someone might say, "Josh, it sounds to me like everything you are saying here is for addicts. That's not me. I just like to look now and then. I'm not even close to that level! It's no big deal."

Make no mistake! While God is in the forgiving, healing, cleansing and renewing business, pornography is nothing to mess with. I saw an online picture of one of the missionaries we support in Asia, and she's sitting there stroking a tiger. We all know that in the natural, you don't just sit there and pet tigers! Obviously, this cat was probably drugged up on sedatives, and/or stuffed with a huge meal just before this picture was taken so that the animal isn't the least bit hungry, but ready to go into a food coma. Well, don't be foolish about porn; when you deal with this issue lightly, you are stroking a starving tiger! You're sitting next to something you don't want to be dealing with, when very shortly you wake up, and the consequences are tearing you apart. Let God help you be completely free.

Here's another big lie: "Everyone I know is secretly viewing pornography."

I want to say this very carefully, because I do not in any way view myself as "Holier than thou." The fact that I'm a pastor doesn't make me holier than anybody. I have said this earlier, that the worst decision of my life was to surrender my virginity before I married my wife Anna, and if I had known the amazing wife that God was giving me, there is no way I would have made the decisions I made as a promiscuous teenager. But I do not view pornography.

Do I wear that as some kind of badge of honor? No. Are there pop-ups that have ambushed me and I've lingered at? Yes. Are there movie scenes where I fast-forwarded past, but not fast enough? Yes. Do I have temptations of lust that cross my mind? Of course! In fact, to be totally transparent, while writing this book I felt an unprecedented amount of temptation and attack to discredit this area of my life. It led me to look to my pastor and best friend for some extra accountability and covering.

But for all of us, so much is at stake! How could I help anyone with moral authority if porn was something I sought out and medicated myself with? If you are dabbling with it or trapped in it, it's tempting to accept the lie that everybody you know is looking at pornography. This lie will break you down. It says "What's the big deal? Everybody's doing it! Heck, my leaders are probably doing it!" No, everybody is NOT doing it, and you don't have to either! That's not spoken to increase the guilt and shame on those who *are* struggling with it. You may have victory in other areas that I struggle with and vice versa. We're on this journey into a life of victory together, but we won't get there believing lies or accepting excuses.

4. Accept God's Forgiveness

> Psalm 51:16-17 (NIV)
> *You do not delight in sacrifice, or I would bring it;*
> *you do not take pleasure in burnt offerings.*
> *The sacrifices of God are a broken spirit;*
> *a broken and contrite heart, O God, you will not despise.*

"God, You don't want me to beat myself. You don't want me whipping myself. You get no joy out of a sacrifice like that, or I would bring You one."

The only sacrifice that is required for you is the one already offered by Jesus Christ. His victory on the cross not only paid for the penalty of sin against you, bringing forgiveness; it also broke the power of sin within you, giving you freedom. Sometimes we talk of the cross only in the context of the penalty He paid. Thank God Jesus DID pay my penalty. If our faith is in His work on the cross, we are NOT going to hell because of His payment of death. It wasn't just the penalty that He took, however. He also took the power of your sin to the cross!

Our sin is strong but His grace is stronger.

CONQUERABLE

Pornography is NOT an all-powerful, unbeatable giant! Is it an unavoidable issue and challenge? Yes. Is it a widespread problem? Yes. Is it extremely dangerous, addictive and harmful? Yes. Is the road to recovery incredibly costly and long and difficult, requiring lots of support? Yes.

Is it unbeatable? NOT A CHANCE! Jesus' victory did two things: He paid the penalty, and He broke the power. One gives us forgiveness. One gives us freedom. This is the gospel!
You can know all of the biological reasons and logical reasons for not looking at porn, but the only fix for the issue is to lay hold of the spiritual and moral victory won through Jesus Christ.

WHAT'S AT STAKE IS BIGGER THAN OURSELVES?

There is much more at stake here with this issue than your personal purity. You have something much bigger to fight for!

Did you ever go walking through the woods with others, one after another, when all of a sudden the person in front is confronted by a small, bendable branch across the path? That person starts to push the branch forward carefully so that they can walk by it.

Sometimes, he bends it in order to get by himself and then releases it, only to smack the next person in line. That could happen simply because the person was careless, but then again sometimes when I was growing up my siblings did that to me just because they didn't like me! The branch may have prickers on it too, or it may not, but the impact is felt by the next person in line.

Sometimes the person in front is careful and holds it up so the next person can get by easily.

It's an even better practice, however, to cut that branch off! What gets healed in us won't be handed down (generationally) through us.

When it comes to generational strongholds, you have the power not only to defeat pornography for yourself, but to break off the impurity for the sake of generations after you. The decision to get on a road to recovery is a legacy decision. You have an opportunity to set in motion a current of purity that leaves an incredible spiritual heritage for those coming after you.

As generations move through the forest of sexual temptation, no matter what the people up the line from you have done, you have the opportunity to love the people down the line with your private decisions. As you move forward on the path to victory, you are cutting that branch off for your children and the others that you influence.

Churches all over the world are using the "Conquer Series – A Battle Plan for Purity" (conquerseries.com) to help men and women regarding this issue. I highly recommend the series. One of the presenters said this:

> "What a person does in life becomes their history. What they set in motion for others becomes their legacy."
> **Paul Cole**

What will be your legacy of purity?

I walk in sexual purity to the best I possibly can. I do so for my God, for myself, for my wife, for my boys, for my church family, and for my ministry to the greater Body of Christ.

Somebody said: "Josh, just you addressing this issue is like smacking the bees nest and making them mad. You better be careful. The devil is going to put a target on your back."

Hey, I already have a target on my back, and so do you, because there is more at stake than us! While the devil may be out to get us, the greater reality is that our Father is out to keep us! God loves me more than the devil could ever hate me.

He can show us why we were even looking and reaching out for these images, what the "lack" or desire for affirmation was, and what the root issue in the soul was that He can heal. Pain seeks pleasure. He's the only one who can satisfy.

With my whole heart, I know that His grace is much more powerful than sin and that love is more powerful than lust.

I want to suggest a prayer:

Jesus, I believe that my sexual sin may be strong, but Your grace is stronger. I believe that You died, not only to pay the penalty of my sin but to break the power of my sin. I accept You as my Savior. I also need You to be my deliverer. Grant a willing spirit within me to sustain me, and the willpower to partner with the Holy Spirit's power.

"Shame, if left unchecked, can take root and become a core part of our identity. It creates a false identity that affects our perception, keeping us a prisoner in our mind. Shame is a thief."

PAUL MANWARING[5]

05

SHAME OFF YOU

When discussing the inner complexities of the human soul there is really no better place to turn for advice than to an ugly ogre named Shrek and his relentlessly chatty side kick "Donkey."

"For your information, there is a lot more to ogres than people think. Ogres are like onions," Shrek explained.

Quicker than an ogre can think, Donkey starts blurting, "They stink? They make you cry? Oh, you leave 'em out in the sun, they get all brown and start sprouting little white heads?"

"No… No … NO! Layers! Onions have layers. Ogres have layers. Onions have layers. You get it? We both have layers."

Donkey persists, "Oh, you both have layers. Not everybody likes onions… Cakes! Cakes have layers. Everybody likes cakes."

"I don't care what everybody likes. Ogres are not like cakes."[6]

People are like onions. We have layers! I do and you do. There are layers of complexity in regard to how we are made up, body, soul and spirit. What you see on the outside is not the real picture of who we really are.

It's important to address the very delicate topic of shame so that we can be free to live in the fullness of what the gospel of Jesus Christ has already purchased for us.

Shame is the unwanted friend that all of us have kept company with at some time.

Shame is an unspoken epidemic. No one likes to talk about it and usually the more shame you carry through life, the less you are willing to talk about it.

There is an interesting dilemma you face if you listen to what researchers say, because according to their data everyone deals with some level of shame … everyone except those who are incapable of feeling it, and those are called "Sociopaths." Isn't it nice to know that you are in one of these two categories:

1. Yes, I grapple with some level of shame, or
2. No, I am incapable of feeling shame and am therefore a sociopath!

THE SWAMP CALLED "SHAME"

Everyone deals with shame at some point. The key is to overcome it. The topic is so wildly relatable that when research professor Brené Brown spoke about the subject in a TED Talk, it quickly went viral.[7] It is one of the most viewed TED Talks ever. Brown explains that shame is like a huge swampland of the soul. Nobody wants to live in, camp at, or hang out in a swamp. You have to trek through and keep going. It's not a pleasant place to stay.

You have to process shame, not live there. You can't just say "I'm going to get around it or pretend it's not there." Because of what Jesus did you certainly don't have to leave shame unchecked, set up a home or live there, but you can't start a new chapter in life if you keep going back and re-reading and re-experiencing the last chapter.

Dr. Brown did her PhD research on the subject of shame and has written extensively on it. She describes it this way: *"Shame is the intensely painful experience or mindset of believing you are flawed and, therefore, unworthy of acceptance and belonging."*

Acceptance and belonging are two things we all need.

Shame is not just a topic for psychologists and researchers; it's all through the Bible, from Genesis to Christ.

> Genesis 2:25 (NIV)
> *The man and his wife were both naked, and they felt no shame.*

This kind of "shame-free living" was God's design from the very beginning. That's why this book is so important and why I chose the name "Overcome." His will is not that you only experience "Mildly Successful Shame Management." His will is shame-free living as the overcomer that He designed you to be.

We were created for connection and for engaging with God and with people. Shame blows up the bridge of connection or damages even the possibility of engaging in the most life-giving relationships possible, either with Him or with others.

A friend of mine told me of his toddler son who was very sensitive about wrong-doing and desperately wanted always to please his parents even from that early age. Wandering alone into the kitchen one day, he dropped and broke a dish and felt so ashamed that instead of telling his parents about the accident, he quietly and through tears was trying to pick up the evidence of his dropped dish. My friend walked into the kitchen a couple of minutes later and found his little boy sitting on the floor with tears streaming down his cheek and with bleeding hands from trying to pick up the sharp shreds of glass resulting from the accident. This father felt awful that his little boy was literally bleeding shame unnecessarily and was too embarrassed to invite his daddy in to make it all better.

About two years later that same boy was outside with his older sister but then seemed to disappear, to the horror of his mother. She couldn't find him anywhere; despite calling out, he wouldn't answer. Her heart raced as she called his name inside the house, upstairs, then downstairs, out on the porch. She called for him outside, but still with no answer. Back in the house, lifting her voice again but still with no answer, she thought "Oh God, what has happened to my son?"

About to call 911 she heard a sniff, and then another. Following the muffled cries to a back bedroom, there he was, behind the bed in the corner of the room crying.

"What's wrong?" the mother asked and reached for him. Out came the story of how he had accidentally run his tricycle into the neighbor's parked car and scratched it.

It reminds me of the human tendency to bleed internally over mistakes, mistreatments, sins and past situations, when all the while our heavenly Father is longing to come, pick up the broken pieces, bring comfort, and give assurance of His love and acceptance.

When you were young, did you ever misbehave and react with a "Daddy, don't come in here" or, "Mommy, don't look at me! Look away." Adam and Eve hid from God out of fear and shame.

As we grow out of childhood we may not use those words anymore, but often the attitude of our heart is to say internally "God, look away right now. I don't want You to become ashamed of who I've become or what I've done."

All through the Scriptures about shame, it deals with what is supposed to be a great connection, an eye-to-eye relationship with the Lord, and our countenance in the face of God. Always in Scripture there is a turning away when it comes to shame. People turn their face away, saying "God, don't look at me right now!" God is never turning away. It's us!

Even national leaders in the Bible feel shame because of their nation's actions. It's the kind of shame that you can carry for your own people when you live in an ungodly culture.

Ezra 9:6 (NIV)
"I am too ashamed and disgraced, my God, to lift up my face to you, because our sins are higher than our heads and our guilt has reached to the heavens.

There's also an individual turning away that comes from feeling weighed down by the brokenness of shame. Notice the countenance of the person's face mentioned in these two passages.

Psalm 44:15 (NIV)
I live in disgrace all day long, and my face is covered with shame

Psalm 69:16-20 (NIV)
Answer me, Lord, out of the goodness of your love;
in your great mercy turn to me.
Do not hide your face from your servant; answer me quickly,
for I am in trouble.
Come near and rescue me; deliver me because of my foes.
You know how I am scorned, disgraced and shamed;
all my enemies are before you.
Scorn has broken my heart and has left me helpless;
I looked for sympathy, but there was none, for comforters,
but I found none.

David articulates feelings we've all had in this Psalm. Have you ever felt when you are going through tough times "Nobody has a clue what I'm going through?" He also grasps very common shame-based fears. Ironically, shame fears the very isolation that it creates! When struggling with shame there comes a longing and a tendency to isolate yourself, but then you fear that very same isolation and loneliness.

It's so important to understand shame in order to experience the overcoming life that God intends and to grasp the major difference between guilt and shame.

"Guilt" focuses on behavior. Guilt says, "I did something wrong. I apologize. I made a mistake. I'm sorry."

> **"Shame is like wearing already forgiven sins like a name tag."**
>
> PAUL SCANLON

"Shame" on the other hand is an inaccurate focus on self. It doesn't say "My bad. Forgive me for what I did." Shame owns it on an identity level and says "I am bad. I am a mistake." In shame, you apologize for your presence, for the air you breath and the space you take up in the lives of others. That's why you pull away from that space, from the time and space you take in people's lives, and even from the space you take in God's life. You pull away from the very connection and relationships that you ought to be strengthened by as you carry shame on an identity level.

Shame is highly connected to a diversity of human problems: addictions of all kinds, anger, violence, inappropriate levels of teasing and bullying, suicide, eating disorders and cutting.

While shame may feel similar for everyone, sometimes we organize it differently in our minds. For some people, shame often appears as an unattainable web of conflicting expectations as to who you are supposed to be. There's a struggle with perceptions, demands, standards and "molds" as to who you think you should be. Others process it all differently. Their primary mindset may be "Don't be perceived as being weak! Don't show emotion. Suppress your expressions. Stuff 'em."

For both men and women, we need to be constantly reminded that being vulnerable and showing emotion is actually a sign of good health. I've known people from both genders who have said things like "I don't want to cry" or "I've got to keep it together."

In the medical community, newborn babies don't get a break. As soon as you were born, as a baby, you were given a test, the Apgar Test. I'm all for good health, but a test five seconds after you've come through that kind of trauma? When my son Jesse was born two weeks late, he was large, 9 lbs, blue and kind of smurf-look-

> **"Feelings buried alive don't die."**
>
> ABI STUMVALL

ing. The doctors and nurses were handing him back and forth, prodding, poking, writing notes down, checking things out... no slack for the little guy! How do you pass the Apgar Test and prove good health? By doing what? Crying! Taking in air and letting it out. Emotional expression is a good thing.

Sometimes even anger is a sign of health, depending on the situation. If you have been a victim, and your safe emotional boundaries have been crossed, you may live in a pattern of passivity. It is possible to shut emotions down in an unhealthy way. We've got to say "Yes" to the emotions that God gave us to help us.

SHAME AND THE LAW OF GOD

What I am about to share with you in the remainder of this chapter may be one of the most powerful parts of this book for you.

Much of the shame people feel comes from not understanding God's law. God is holy; His ways are just. His Word is pure and His standards are high. So how do I relate to God's law without feeling guilt or shame?

> Romans 3:20 (NIV)
> *For no one can ever be made right with God by doing what the law commands. The law simply shows us how sinful we are.*

God says if you break one of His commands you are guilty of all of them. You can't "be good enough" to not be "Guilty." As novel as this idea may be to you, He didn't give us the law because He had this naïve idea that we could do it. After Adam and Eve ate of the tree, their eyes were open to the knowledge of good and evil and of right and wrong. God wanted to show us how desperately we need Him, so that the relationship could be restored on a right foundation of what is true!

The law was not given so we could become more perfect. Self-perfection is not the goal of the human experience. Relationship with God is the goal.

> Romans 6:14
> *Sin is no longer your master, for you no longer live under the requirements of the law. Instead, you live under the freedom of God's grace.*

Realize that just as the power of grace is so far superior to the law, so are the expectations under grace. Under the law I had to murder you to be guilty. Under grace, I only have to get mad and call you a bad name and I'm guilty. I've never had a strong desire to murder, but I have gotten really mad in my heart and called people names. Under the law, I had to commit adultery to be guilty, but under grace I just have to look at a woman with lust and I've committed adultery in my heart.

Knowing the law, knowing right from wrong, knowing good from bad ... all of that is POWERLESS to help us fulfill the expectations of that knowledge. Grace empowers us so much more, but how does this work? The title of this book is "Overcome" for a reason. How do you overcome?

In Romans 7 Paul says that we have entered into a "new marriage!" As long as a person is alive their spouse is bound to them. But if their spouse dies, they are free to marry another. The 10 Commandments God gave to Moses on Mt. Sinai were coupled with 613 moral and ceremonial laws. There was no way anyone could keep them all, which produced all of this guilt and shame because people failed to keep the law. As God's Old Testament people, you were in covenant with God, "married" if you will, to that Law as long as you lived. The only way out of the contract with this incredibly burdensome system of laws and that "covenant marriage," is death. Now the Law, that "spouse," if you will, isn't going to die anytime soon. "Til heaven and earth passes away" these laws are not passing away.[8]

The great news is this! Paul explains further that when you placed your faith in Christ, you "died" to that old marriage and now you are married to another, even to Christ Himself.

Oftentimes when someone is wanting to end an awkward relationship they will say "It's not you. It's me." Sometimes there will be some hurt. The other person won't believe them and think "they are trying to lie their way out of this relationship when down deep they just don't like me" (not that I would have had any experience on awkward relationships, of course).

"No no. I mean it! It's not you. It's me," the person breaking it off will say again.

When it comes to the marriage of God's people with the Law, the truth really is: "The problem is with us, not with Him." To my flesh, the Law seems so demanding and perfectionist and accusatory, yet in reality the Law is really very good and very holy. There was nothing wrong with the Law. We just couldn't match up. Can you imagine being married to such a perfect spouse?

When married to the Law, you are married to the perfect spouse and just standing next to that, you would automatically feel bad about yourself, ashamed of who you were in comparison. Our imperfections standing next to His perfection is a difficult marriage to be in. It's not that there was something wrong with the law; there was something wrong with us!

We celebrate water baptism precisely because, when our faith is in Jesus Christ the Son of God, we "died" to our previous marriage to the Law. That covenant relationship was done, severed, and broken. By identifying with Christ's death and as we died with Him, we have been released from that marriage and are now free to marry another, even Christ Himself who is the embodiment of grace and truth.

Being married to Christ is a completely different marriage atmosphere than being married to the Law. The Old Testament prophets even spoke of what really happens: Jesus writes the law on your heart. We fulfill His commands now because we love Him, not because we have to try to do so in our own human strength. It's no longer a love for the law but the law of love that governs our behavior. As we love Jesus, it becomes natural to obey His commandments and standards.

Yes, Jesus will still challenge and provoke us to come up higher but the Lord isn't there rebuking us right and left, telling us what we are not. He's reminding us again and again what we were created and meant to be.

> Romans 8:1-2
> *So now there is no condemnation for those who belong to Christ Jesus. And because you belong to him, the power of the life-giving Spirit has freed you from the power of sin that leads to death.*

The word "NOW" is significant. Now that we're in a new marriage, now that we're in a life-giving relationship with Christ where He lives in us and we walk with Him, now we can draw on the power of Christ in us. The Ten Commandments of Mt. Sinai brought bondage and death, but in the New Testament we are called to Mt. Zion, to the presence of God, and to a relationship with God that brings freedom. At the giving of the Law 3,000 people died. At the giving of the Holy Spirit in the New Testament, 3,000 people were born again to new life. On Mt. Sinai, the clouds descended and mountains rumbled with loud noise and fire all around. On Pentecost in the new marriage, the Holy Spirit descended and there was the loud sound of a rushing mighty wind and tongues of fire. For Israel, the Law was written on tablets of stone. For those who will place their trust in Christ, the law is written on the human heart.

On the old mountain, the rules were broken even before they got carried from the top of the mountain to the people below. There was no power embedded within the law itself to help us carry out the commands. In the new marriage, our new spouse provides all the power.

> "Grace empowers us to do what truth demands."
> **John Bevere**

In the United States, our Congressmen or Senators can pass laws and write them on paper and end up breaking the laws themselves. You can post the rules in classrooms, businesses and restaurants but the rules themselves cannot give you the power to keep them. The Ten Commandments really aren't that hard, but without the power of the Holy Spirit they are impossible. I'm so glad that by dying to the Law we can be married to the resurrected Christ, and be transformed by His power into overcomers.

What Value Does the Law Have in My Life?:
It WAS my master.

According to Galatians 3:24, the Law was our master or tutor to bring us to Christ. "Was" is the operative word there, as in "past tense."

Who was the "Master" or "Tutor?"

This was powerful imagery Paul used when he wrote these words to the culture of that day. The master or tutor was a person that the family hired to take care of their young boy from age 6 to 16 years old, and the sole job of that person was to watch over that boy, making sure he got to school and back home safely.

The job of the master was to lead the child to the teacher.

The value of the Law, as our master or tutor, is to lead us safely to the Teacher, Jesus Christ Himself, whom we desperately need. Being so imperfect, it wouldn't take long being married to the "perfect" spouse known as the Law, for us say "Get me out of that relationship! I need Jesus."

Galatians 3:23-26

Before the way of faith in Christ was available to us, we were placed under guard by the law. We were kept in protective custody, so to speak, until the way of faith was revealed.

Let me put it another way. The law was our guardian until Christ came; it protected us until we could be made right with God through faith. And now that the way of faith has come, we no longer need the law as our guardian. For you are all children of God through faith in Christ Jesus.

The law was our "guardian" or master or tutor, until we could safely acknowledge that to be right with God, we needed Christ.

What Value Does the Law Have in My Life?:

It IS my mirror.

The law is my mirror. "Is" is the operative word there. This is present tense.

James 1:22-25

Do not merely listen to the word, and so deceive yourselves. Do what it says. Anyone who listens to the word but does not do what it says is like someone who looks at his face in a mirror and, after looking at himself, goes away and immediately forgets what he looks like. But whoever looks intently into the perfect law that gives freedom, and continues in it—not forgetting what they have heard, but doing it—they will be blessed in what they do.

We are not saved by the perfect Law, but we are *blessed* by it!

Let me add this important distinction. The Law beautifully reflects the boundaries of God's desires, but it does not reflect the boundaries of His love.

What do I mean? Check out this test. Does everyone in the world keep God's beautiful and perfect laws? Of course not, no way, not even close. But does God love the whole world? Yes! "For God so loved the whole world."[9] Approval and acceptance are two very different things. That's why we can have grace for friends, children, classmates, and co-workers living a lifestyle far from God's law, truth or safe boundaries. Can I love them? Yes, I can love lawbreakers. I may not approve of the lifestyle. Their choices may be contrary to wisdom, harmful and foolish, but I can still love them. I may not approve of your actions and lifestyle choices because they are outside of the parameters of God's Law, but you are never outside the parameters of God's love.

If we all in the family of God walk free of our own shame and get a handle on this perspective on shame and the Law, we're all going to start handing out the love of God at a whole new level.

SILENCING THE VOICE OF SHAME

So, if the Law WAS our master, and it IS our mirror, and I'm in a new marriage relationship with Jesus Christ, how can I now silence the voice of shame? How do you silence the voice that says things to your mind like this:

- *I know what happened to you as a child!*
- *I know what you look at!*
- *I know what you fantasize about!*
- *I know what you've touched, drank, consumed, did!*
- *I know why your spouse left you!*
- *I know the real reason you are still single!*
- *I know why you never finished your degree!*
- *I know why you strive to be perfect and powerful!*
- *I know how you feel that your dad never paid attention to you even when you made the dean's list or became CFO!*
- *I know about your bankruptcy!*
- *I know how your parenting mistakes messed up your kid's life!*

Shame is that gremlin talking and talking on the inside of you, looking for agreement with every accusation.

Shame is a radio station that is always playing, and it plays the two "greatest hits" continuously. These are the two greatest hits that play in the minds of people everywhere. These hits are sung in every language, culture, people and in every generation! The first of these two songs is titled "Never good enough!" And if you are able to defeat it and get that song turned off, you'll hear the second song, "Who do you think you are?" Come on! Wouldn't you like to silence these two songs in your soul?

Back to an illustration from Brené Brown. From her extensive studies on shame, she said that if you put shame into a Petri dish (remember those from science lab?), there are three conditions that help shame grow exponentially: Secrecy, Silence, and Judgment. If you are struggling with some shame and you add in some secrecy, and then put in a dash of silence, and pour on a little judgment, the shame grows exponentially.

Be encouraged! There is an antidote that is like a herbicide to weeds: Empathy. If you take that same amount of shame but douse it with this one thing, empathy, that shame will begin to die. Pour on some grace-filled, truth-filled empathy, and shame cannot survive.

> **"Vulnerability, many times, is the most accurate measure of our courage. You can choose comfort or courage but not both. Vulnerability is the birthplace of creativity, innovation, and change."**
>
> **BRENÉ BROWN**[11]

People can't express empathy for you about the shame or guilt you are dealing with if they have no idea it's happening. It's why God calls us as believers to family and to community. There is no empathy without relationship, and no empathy without a choice to be vulnerable. Vulnerability kills shame.

Know this! Vulnerability is NOT weakness! That is a profoundly dangerous myth. Some might say, "If I say this or do this I'll be viewed as weak or broken." Actually, vulnerability takes courage. You'll hear the voice of shame speak to you as you're opening up to someone saying, "What do you think you are doing?" That little mind gremlin is again trying to keep you isolated and bound in shame.

The truth is that vulnerability brings both healing to you and hope to others. The ironic thing is that when we witness someone else being vulnerable and transparent, we don't consciously think "What weakness!" We don't get disgusted; we actually saw it as a positive step when someone else took it! We recognize the bravery. So, when the situation is ours, we can't give into the lie that we'll appear weak if we open up to the light.

The word "empathy" sometimes gets a bad rap. "Too much empathy and they'll just stay in their sin," someone might say. Actually, Kingdom empathy empowers people to get OUT of their sin.

> "Kingdom accountability calls people up into their identity not just out on their sin."
> **Graham Cooke**

We all need to hear "same here" more than we need to hear "you should." Because shame is shrouded and fostered in secrecy, there is usually a deep sense of feeling alone in the struggle with it. So let me help with a whole list of "same here's." In meetings and conversations as a pastor over the years people have come up to me and said things like the following, and I just want to say to each one "same here." And I want to say to you, "I get it." And whether you think it's possible or not, "I've been there too."

"Josh, I have …"

- "Buried some past wounds foolishly hoping that time would heal them." Same here.
- "Made major mistakes raising my kids, and I think I messed them up." Yup, same here.
- "Struggled with eating too much and I feel so ashamed." For sure. I've had seconds on dessert after kids go to bed so they wouldn't know. (Anna and I call it "parent tax.")
- "Eye-guzzled Netflix 3 or 4 episodes in a row and wonder, *What am I doing with my life!*" Same here.
- "Committed some serious sexual sins before I surrendered to Christ that

affect me today." Same here.

- "Struggled with sexual sins and temptations after becoming a Christian and I'm ashamed." Same here.
- "Made some significant financial blunders." I'm in that club too.

That is how healing and hope happens. We receive forgiveness from God. Jesus' half brother James also taught us that we get healing when we confess our sins to each other (James 5:16). You and I have power over what we can talk about. Empathy is not so that further sin and shame can be excused. Kingdom empathy never does that. Kingdom empathy empowers people to bring shame to the light and out in the open where it will be overcome. If you feel like you do not have a person in your life who can say "same here" for you, then start being that voice to others in your path and watch how God starts to give back to you.

I'm not sure how two animated movies made it into the same chapter of this book (and now you know that as well as being a preacher, I'm a father with young kids), but there are some incredible lyrics from the Disney movie *Frozen* in the song "Let it Go."

Don't let them in, don't let them see
Be the good girl you always have to be
Conceal, don't feel, don't let them know
Well now they know
Let it go, let it go
Can't hold it back anymore
Let it go, let it go

All of us need to let go of our shame. We've got to let go of our past, stop coming into agreement and rehearsing that shameful voice that says, "Not enough" or "Who do you think you are?" We've got to have some courage and humility and vulnerability to kill the power of shame, and let's learn to talk to ourselves like we would talk to someone we actually … LOVE! Let's declare "I'm in a new relationship, a new marriage, a new covenant, a new

Spirit inside me of me and I can begin to walk with God and NOT turn my face from Him."

Letting go makes sure that the mind gremlin of shame is no longer doing any back seat driving in the recesses of your brain.

My shame, my "Petri dish" may look different than yours, but the solutions are still the same.

Because of Jesus' work on the cross, we no longer have to bring old mindsets into new seasons.

Hebrews 12:2 (NIV)
fixing our eyes on Jesus, the pioneer and perfecter of faith. For the joy set before him he endured the cross, scorning its shame, and sat down at the right hand of the throne of God.

Jesus took your shame and mine, and despised it to its face. In a very real sense, He shamed shame! All the things you try to hide from Him He already faced. Jesus already faced all the shame that needs to be faced. He hung naked on a cursed tree on a hill outside a city for all to see, all for my shame and for yours. Why would we want to pick it back up and keep carrying it? He says, "Shame ON ME, and shame OFF you." That's God's way. It's the way we overcome.

Isaiah 50:7 (NIV)
Because the Sovereign Lord helps me, I will not be disgraced. Therefore, have I set my face like flint and I know I will not be put to shame.

WHEN SHAME IS NO LONGER YOUR NAME

"The ghosts of all the people you used to be are proud of who you've become and thank you for letting them go. All those former versions of you would like to thank you for not mistaking them as the final you. They don't miss you, need to hear from

David had just become king. In the wake of King Saul and Jonathan's death, David wanted to honor someone from their household. Enter Mephibosheth. This man is originally introduced, not by his name, but by his issue.

"He is crippled in both feet."

What a terrible way to live, having your issue be your introduction. You enter a room and immediately imagine what people must be thinking. You begin a conversation with someone and your own thoughts condemn you. You know what you've done. You know what's been done to you.

Mephibosheth was just five years old when the tragic report came in that King Saul and his son, Jonathan, had died on the battlefield. In fear, his nurse picked him up and began to run. As she fled, however, she tripped and dropped the young boy. That fall not only injured Mephibosheth's feet forever, but it also impaired his identity.

For Jonathan, King Saul's son and David's best friend, was Mephibosheth's father. On that one defining day, Mephibosheth lost both his father and his *future*. What's even worse is that shame was pronounced over him every time his name was uttered.

Mephibo in the Hebrew language means "out of my mouth," and *sheth* means "shame or embarrassment." Every time his name was mentioned, by himself or others, Mephibosheth was showered with shame and reminded of his victimhood.

But then grace entered his story. And grace, my friend, is always more powerful than shame.

King David invited Mephibosheth to come and eat at his table. David wanted to honor someone who would have easily been overlooked and most certainly mistreated. The word honor means "to value." David wanted to value someone whom others would have been quick to dismiss and despise.

Mephibosheth entered the king's glorious hall with great fear. He likely would have hung his head low to avoid eye contact. He referred to himself before the king as a worthless "dead dog." His self-image was swallowed up by shame.

His grandfather, the previous king, had betrayed King David.

His father was dead.

He was a "worthless" cripple.

Mephibosheth was not only a cripple, he was a victim. His injury was caused by someone else's error. The longer a person allows shame to define them, the more likely they are to allow the identity of a powerless victim to enslave them also.

What use was Mephibosheth to the king now? Why would David choose to show favor to him, let alone have him dine at his own table?

> **"Honor is when you can celebrate who a person is without stumbling over who they are not."**
>
> BILL JOHNSON

Thankfully, we never have to take an old mindset into a new season.

David's gesture is an unexpected and beautiful picture of New Testament grace hidden within an Old Testament story.

Mephibosheth would have been carried into the palace due to his disability. Every time he sat at the king's table, however, his crippled feet were out of sight and covered. Completely covered. He sat as a son. He sat as one of the king's own children and heirs would do. Mephibosheth dined there regularly for the rest of his life, his disability and shame swallowed up by the generous invitation of the king.

Being carried to the table is another prophetic picture of grace that is extended to all mankind through the cross of Christ. Who do you know who could ever earn by their merit a place at King Jesus' table? Yet, when we take our rightful place, our shame, our "issues," our previous identity and poor self-image are all covered over by grace. We become children, not just of a king, but of the King of Kings.

None of this is by our own effort. This invitation and new identity is a result of Jesus' extravagant grace.

Shame is no longer our name.

Victimhood is no longer our story.

"Many times it looks like God is killing a leader when He is actually growing one."

KEVIN MYERS

06

WINNING WITHIN:
CHARACTER STRONGER
THAN OUR HORMONES

Football season is one of my favorite times of the year. I'll get together with some friends, we go to whoever's house has the best and biggest flat screen TV, and have our little fantasy football league so we can trash talk each other. We might be kind of quiet as we watch the game until the running back on my fantasy football team breaks out for a 60-yard gain. In that moment when I realize that my team's place in the fantasy league standings just took a giant leap forward I get amped! I'm about to have even more reason to talk smack to my competitors. It's a great moment for sure. I've been known to even leap up off the couch and do a very uncoordinated dance while I am lost in that moment of sweet momentum. Of course, that exhilarating bliss is short-lived when you hear those dreaded words from the play-by-play announcer, "It's coming back."

The yellow flag on the play indicates that there's been some infraction, some violation of the rules in a moment of indiscretion that causes all of that momentum to be lost. Not only does the 60-yard gain not count as forward progress, now the team is actually being moved backwards! The referees don't just bring the football back to where you started; my guys lost yardage. There will be no highlight reel tape for ESPN to show off my favorite running back.

This can happen in life. At work and in business, profits may be up, the market is good, and all of a sudden one unwise lack of discretion or poor decision can cause you to lose everything. It can happen in politics or in any area of our lives.

We can be moving forward in our lives with tremendous forward momentum, but if there is a breakdown of character it can all come back. Your gifting, talents, abilities and even the anointing upon your life (the calling that He has placed upon you) can take you places that your character cannot sustain. That's why God is in the business of character development. He wants to pour out so much blessing and favor upon you, and release so much influence through your life, but he doesn't want it to explode like so often happens.

A LEADER IN THE MAKING

There is a credibility crisis in the world. We've had presidents of nations apologizing for themselves and for scandals in their administrations. Let's not personally add more to the integrity debt that we see our culture carrying.

Joseph of the Old Testament had a clear sense of calling from an early age. As it turns out, it would be neither his advantages or disadvantages that would produce fruit, but the calling of God. He was one of 12 princes, a great grandson of Abraham, in a wealthy but imperfect family. Those benefits could not in themselves bring to pass his calling, nor could the reality of his family's dysfunctions hold him back. God had to bring him to a place of utter dependency upon the Lord.

There were seasonal process events that formed him, high mountaintop experiences and some of the darkest valley lows recorded in Scripture. These process events are what Chuck Swindoll calls "a series of great opportunities brilliantly disguised as impossible situations."

At the high points Joseph saw the acts of God and at the low points he learned the ways of God. From the prophetic dream highs to the lows of a pit into which his brothers cast him, from the exhilarating rescue out of the pit to being sold as a slave, from the mountaintop of being promoted over all of Potiphar's house, to being "asked for coffee" by Potiphar's wife and being thrown into prison, and from being promoted again over the prison to being forgotten by those he helped … through it all, God's favor was the overriding factor that kept propelling Joseph forward into the purposes of God. On display in this account is the kindness of God developing the character of His sons and daughters, the same kindness that He has towards you.

> **"Every time He touches your life to break you, He runs the risk of making you."**
>
> DAN MOHLER

Pastor Kevin Myers says, "Many times it looks like God is *killing* a leader when He is actually *growing* one."

If we want to finish the race as winners in the faith fulfilling the call of God on our lives, we can't just envision where we want to go and what we want to do. We have to figure out first what kind of person we need to become! If character doesn't get developed, we can't win within.

When Satan touches a believer he takes a great risk. The devil is a gambler. Our enemy is hoping is that the temptation or trial he sends will arouse our flesh. What he fears is that the very same temptation may actually awaken our character and dependence on God.

Even as a slave, Joseph was one of the richest people in all of Egypt because he maintained his character. Character is more valuable than gold. Character is more empowering than advantageous circumstances.

Billy Graham said this about character, "When wealth is lost, nothing is lost; when health is lost, something is lost; when character is lost, all is lost!"

Genesis 39:1-6

When Joseph was taken to Egypt by the Ishmaelite traders, he was pur-
chased by Potiphar, an Egyptian officer. Potiphar was captain of the
guard for Pharaoh, the king of Egypt. The Lord was with Joseph, so he
succeeded in everything he did as he served in the home of his Egyptian
master. Potiphar noticed this and realized that the Lord was with Jo-
seph, giving him success in everything he did. This pleased Potiphar, so
he soon made Joseph his personal attendant. He put him in charge of
his entire household and everything he owned. From the day Joseph was
put in charge of his master's household and property, the Lord began to
bless Potiphar's household for Joseph's sake. All his household affairs ran
smoothly, and his crops and livestock flourished. So Potiphar gave Joseph
complete administrative responsibility over everything he owned. With
Joseph there, he didn't worry about a thing—except what kind of food
to eat!

The favor of God is transferable. You can thrive wherever you are with the favor of God. Joseph was so amazing that Potiphar brought him in the house, released authority to him, and he didn't need to worry about anything except what to eat at dinner!

It's so easy for us, on THIS side of that story, to read the difficulties of his life and think "Joseph, don't sweat it! God has your back! You're being trained to be the Governor of all Egypt, Hallelujah!"

Let's think for a minute though. How many of us have ever been in a job where we didn't understand what God was doing? A boring job in which we complained about the purposelessness of it all? How does Joseph's trial look now from that perspective? Perhaps it's not just a job God has for you either; maybe it's a set up. What if you let your trial become your training?

"Let the tension lead to intention."
Leif Hetland

God knows what He has created and put in you, and He knows how to get it out of you. He may just put you in a situation that you might not even like in order to develop a skill that is buried deep within you.

> "Environment is critical to development."
> **Graham Cooke**

There were skills in Joseph's life that he didn't even know about, that never got put into use until he was put into certain situations. Certain abilities and skills needed to be developed before Joseph could possibly function as the administrator for all of the nation. It is the kindness of God that meticulously tests and develops us to carry greater measures of favor. How do you prepare a young adult to steward enough influence to shape a nation? How do you build the inner infrastructure of a leader in such a way that they won't fold under the weight of favor? Great plans *require* great preparation.

My brother was good enough to help open a door to get me my first job when I was in high school. I was so thankful—thankful, that is, until I actually had to go there and do the job. I was responsible for running the front desk at a real estate office. It came to the point that even in my sleep I was picking up the phone saying "Hi, this is Remax East of the River. How may I help you?" I had to manage eleven separate phone lines coming into that office through this machine. I learned filing and organizing, filled out paperwork, scheduled showings, and helped the agents process things. The Lord was teaching me how to multi-task and succeed in a business setting and I didn't even know it. It wasn't a "trial," it was training!

During Bible School, I got a job managing a grocery store. I had no idea how to run the bakery, the deli, a meat department, the frozen food area, but I was learning to work with and manage people. The Holy Spirit spoke to me "Quit complaining. You are in training." It was my own personal experience in "Potiphar's House."

CHARACTER UP FOR GRABS

There is something different about you. A heathen named Potiphar watched

Joseph and noticed his work ethic, his integrity, his success and how everything he touched turned to gold. "He doesn't carry himself like a slave. There's something different about him." The word used in Scripture to describe Potiphar's response is a word that means this master saw that "Jehovah," the Lord God of the Hebrews, was with Joseph.

How is that possible? Egyptians had many gods. I believe that Potiphar knew who Joseph's God was because Joseph himself witnessed about the Lord. Don't you think that if Potiphar put Joseph in the house over his estate that he also had conversations with Joseph and learned his life story?

Proverbs 10:9 says "He who walks with integrity walks securely." (NKJV) You might think of Joseph, or yourself, as a victim of the decisions and demands of others. It's almost like he was a passive passenger on a wild ride with all kinds of things happening *to* him that he had no choice in. After all, he was:

- "Thrown" into a pit
- "Pulled" out of the pit
- "Sold" to slave traders
- "Purchased" by Potiphar, the captain of Pharaoh's guard
- "Put" in charge in Potiphar's house

Victim? Yes, but that's all about to change once his character is up for grabs!

> Genesis 39:7-18
> *Joseph was a very handsome and well-built young man, and Potiphar's wife soon began to look at him lustfully. "Come and sleep with me," she demanded.*

Lust and love are two totally different things. Lust is all about me. "I want more FROM you than for you! I'm not really concerned about what it will cost you; I want more from you." Love is just the opposite. With love, it's all about you. Love says, "I want more FOR you than from you."

For Joseph, this wasn't just your everyday temptation. This was a serious temptation. Think about his situation. He was in his mid 20's at the peak of a strong young man's sex drive. He's lost relationship with his father and family. If not constantly undergirded with divine perspective and truth, circumstances could easily lead a man to feel like he's even been abandoned by God. He was out of his culture, away from his home language and customs. There was nobody of like heart around, so no sense of accountability to people important in his life, and his father Jacob wasn't around to take him through the book "Every Young Man's Battle" and study it with him. He didn't have the luxury of Bible verses to stand on or a pastor to talk to or church attendance to strengthen him. At this time, there was no wife or kids to disappoint. He was a slave so he had no reputation to ruin. It was a perfect storm scenario! The conditions were perfect for Joseph to blow it!

> **"The world doesn't need better leaders; the world needs better people who lead."**
>
> ERWIN MCMANUS

In some senses, Joseph had nothing to lose by sleeping with the woman. But on the other hand, he had everything to lose. The only thing he had working for him during this time is the internal government of the Holy Spirit. He had within what it took to win.

George Washington said, "Few men have the virtue enough to withstand the highest bidder." We live in a world with some great leaders who know how to get things done, but we need leaders with the moral backing to go along with it. As Erwin McManus said, "The world doesn't need better leaders; the world needs better people who lead."

God has people all over the world that He wants to touch and bless and transform by the power of the gospel. He's preparing a people to serve Him and serve them by developing character so that we can win within and speak with authority. God wanted a man who could serve all of humanity through Egypt's leadership, but he needed a better person to do it and so the training ground for Joseph was developed. God has the perfect training ground for each of us.

HERE COMES A POP QUIZ

You've been there. There's Joseph just doing his job on another normal day. The moment comes when you least expect it, the "Moment of the Maybe." No warnings are given. No opportunity is given to rehearse a response in the "moment of the maybe." He couldn't phone an accountability partner. It's not like she sent him an email or a note down to the slave quarters so that he could think about her advances. She just showed up and reached out. His response came from within, and that's where yours comes from.

Remember the school teacher you hated because all of their tests were "pop quizzes?" Why did they do that? Because they weren't interested in what you could rehearse or cram for. They wanted to see what was inside of you, how their teaching was affecting your base of knowledge.

A pastor friend of mine who lives in a small town tells of a character pop quiz he failed but quickly corrected. He had to run into an office downtown for just a moment a couple of days before Christmas. As he drove up, he saw all the parking spaces were taken within a block away, but there was one space just big enough for his car right in front of that office—by the fire hydrant.

> ### "The testing of your character always comes as a pop-quiz."
>
> ANDY STANLEY

I'll only be one minute, he thought, and he WAS only a minute, except when he came out of the office, there was a police officer writing a ticket.

"Did you realize you parked by that hydrant, Pastor?" the officer asked.

Startled, stunned, afraid to face the consequences, and in a hurry, the pastor answered, "No, sorry," to which the policeman answered, "Okay, never mind, Pastor. Merry Christmas." Then he got back in his police car and drove away with no ticket issued.

Knowing he failed and was going to have to sleep with his conscience, my friend got into his car and followed the policeman until he stopped again (picture that!).

"I'm sorry. I was in a hurry and I lied, officer," my friend confessed. "Please give me that ticket!"

The "moment of the maybe" revealed something in my friend's heart that needed humbling and correction. I guess you could call that secondary opportunity a "make-up quiz." Character tests come the same way as the teachers' pop quizzes, and as we saw in the story, Joseph's character was stronger than his hormones!

But Joseph refused.[12]

What if all the circumstances were removed that would hold you back from temptation? What if you could "get away with it," so to speak. What if you could? Would you?

There's a big difference between an "I can't" and an "I won't." "I cannot" says that if you move all of those limitations from me, then I am there with you and I am all about doing this immoral thing. "I will not" says "Sister, this is never going to happen!"

All the circumstances had already been removed in such a way that it seems Joseph "could've," but he "wouldn't." This wasn't just an "I can't," but it was an "I won't." This wasn't just a "no thanks" but a "NO!" This wasn't just a "no thanks" but a "NO WAY!" I love it. Here is this favor-covered servant of Potiphar and servant of God, and the moment his character is tested, even in a pop quiz, Joseph SLAMMED the door!

Genesis 39:8,9
"Look," he told her, "my master trusts me with everything in his entire household. No one here has more authority than I do. He has held back nothing from me except you, because you are his wife. How could I do such a wicked thing? It would be a great sin against God."

BEHIND THE CURTAIN OF STRONG CHARACTER

#1 | Value the Trust of Others

People in this world need you and they need you to succeed. They need you to win within. How will you win within against the pop quizzes of temptation? Joseph was loyal and valued Potiphar's trust. The master and all the others in the estate counted on him, respected him and depended on him. The pain of giving in to a very momentary pleasure could hurt and impact a lot of people for a long time. We all tend to underestimate the collateral damage of losing in this war.

> Genesis 39:7b,8
> *"Come and sleep with me," she demanded. But Joseph refused. "Look," he told her, "my master trusts me with everything in his entire household.*

What does collateral damage look like? In Bob Reccord's excellent book *Beneath the Surface; Steering Clear of the Dangers that Could Leave you Shipwrecked*[13], there is a gripping email from a 19-year-old girl to her father when she's about to go to college. Her dad has just had an affair and left the family to go be with his girlfriend. Listen to the perspective of this young girl whose father has just squandered his integrity as she expresses it in this email:

> "I cannot comprehend the sincerity of anything you say to me anymore, Dad. You say to me that you love me and yet you knowingly hurt both me and our family. You say that you would die for me and yet you were unwilling to LIVE for me. You say that you miss me and yet it is you who left and abandoned me. I am learning that words are a cheap commodity, especially YOUR words. I am angry with you for living a life of deception, for going against everything you ever taught me to be true and right. I disrespect you as a man, as a husband, and as a father. You are a coward for not being willing to sacrifice something for the love of your own children. More than anything, I pity you. I pity you for throwing your life away for lust. You had everything an earthly man could

ask for: a loving family, two adoring children, a wonderful job, respect in our community, and all the possessions you could ever want. Yet you had a void in your life that, instead of filling it with Christ, you allowed sin to fill it. You are caught inside a cloud of deception. I hurt for you because I know that one day you will look back on your life and realize that you have lost everything for nothing. And I'm afraid for you because I know that God will deal with your sin in His time and it will be far worse than any earthly grief or punishment you could encounter. You are in a dangerous position for not fearing the Lord. I cannot allow you back into my life until you have a change of heart. As much as it hurts me to push you away, it is necessary for my healing. I do not believe that my brother and I are a necessity in your life as you claim. I can recall many times while growing up: you convinced us that you could as a parent desire nothing more than love from your own children. Obviously, you changed your mind. Whether you meant those words in the first place or not, you seem to not have a problem trading us for the replacement of another person. No matter how many times you say that you love me I cannot believe those words without seeing the actions. As disappointed as I am, I will not cease to pray for you. I pray that God will soften your heart. I will pray that you will not find true peace or contentment until you are right with God. I will pray that one day before you die you will have a change of heart and lifestyle and that our relationship can be renewed. I pray that in time God will grant me the grace to forgive you, and in the meantime, I will learn to live again. I will learn to trust and to depend on the Lord as my Father. I'm thankful that God is a Father who won't betray, deceive or hurt me. Life will be different and difficult at times, but I am confident that God will provide for Mom, my brother and me. Each day will get a little easier and a little less painful to face."

Your moment of pleasure will be paid for over many pain-filled years! What a sobering, gut-level email from a 19-year-old daughter to her Dad saying, "What the heck are you doing?" Nobody wants to get a message like that.

Reading this, you may be actually scheming how to take on a fantasy that you've imagined. You think you've counted all of the cost to yourself by moving forward on your plan. My friend, let me assure you that you have underestimated the collateral damage that will result from your decisions if you do.

We get to see in the life of Joseph in Genesis, God lifting the hood over his life and heart, looking inside and saying "Joseph, I'm going to teach you how to win within. I need you to learn this because I cannot even release you to drive into your destiny until that happens."

#2 | Value Your Own Self Worth as God Does

Genesis 39:9
"No one here has more authority than I do."

Identity brings authority. Joseph understood WHO he was, and he understood WHOSE he was. If you understand who you are in Christ and that Christ is who purchased you, certain things will not happen in your life. They are off limits. When you understand the "who" and the "whose," you protect the value, in this case, of yourself. You won't misjudge or abuse yourself.

When it comes to authority for influence, there are always two badges of authority for every parent, leader, teacher, manager, pastor, supervisor, or coach. First there is the badge you wear on the outside, the one everyone sees: the position, authority and title that you have been given. Secondly there is the badge beneath the surface that people don't get to see. They get to feel the effects of it however: the inward, moral authority.[14]

So, Joseph not only respected and valued the trust of Potiphar and others, but he also valued his own self-worth, authority and influence.

#3 | Value the Person Tempting You Even More Than They Value Themself!

Genesis 39:9
"He has held back nothing from me except you, because you are his wife."

Joseph in effect says "Lady, don't you realize that you and only you hold the most sacred office in your husband's life? Nobody in all of Egypt can claim the office that you hold in Potiphar's life!" He honored her value and the value of the institution of marriage even though the married woman did not. There is no more sacred office a person can hold in the life of another than their spouse.

When Anna and I were married, people were excited and having a great time at the reception. At that reception, a girl showed up who had a bit of a crush on me, and because of those feelings she decided to wear a white dress to our wedding. Furthermore, her parents arranged a time for her to do a dance with me at my wedding— an invitation for an entire dance at Anna's and my wedding—from this girl who has a crush on me, wearing a white dress. To hear Anna tell the story, she says it like this: "This was our day, our wedding and nobody is going to steal the attention off the bride and groom! I don't care if that girl WAS only 4 years old!" (I got you, didn't I?) That changes the story a little bit! To this day, Anna says through the laughter: "This was my day, my man, and our moment!"

Seriously, there is something sacred about a relationship of husband and wife. You don't step into that. I don't care who you are. That's sacred territory. Joseph valued that sacred territory, the life of another person. Even when neither party are married, there are gifts God has given you that He wants you to give to your spouse. When we value the sacred life of another human being created special by God, it kills the power of the temptation to use that person for our own momentary gain.

#4 | Value Your Relationship with God!

Your relationship with God is most important. Joseph valued it above all.

Genesis 39: 9 (NLT)
How could I do such a wicked thing? It would be a great sin against God.

Hear the passionate use of "great sin" as he expresses his value for that unbroken relationship with his God. If every other safeguard fails, when you are giving God a fresh, passionate "yes" more than you are giving temptation a resistant "no" to sin, that passionate "yes" will empower you to win with much greater effectiveness than your resistant "no." Joseph didn't mess around with words here. He called it a "wicked" thing and a "great sin."

Scripture gets watered down in our minds sometimes, but God's feelings are clear if you hear His heartbeat. Proverbs says that sexual sin is like drinking sewer water in the street versus drinking water out of your own clean cistern. 1st Corinthians says that your body is home for the Holy Spirit, literally His temple; sexual sin is a sin against your own body, Paul says.

Titus 2 says that His grace teaches us to say "no" to ungodliness. God was training Joseph. Grace empowers you and I to live out what truth demands. Potiphar's wife, however, wasn't having any of it.

STRENGTH AND WISDOM ARE REQUIRED

She kept putting pressure on Joseph day after day, but he refused to sleep with her, and he kept out of her way as much as possible. (Genesis 39:10)

There won't be a season in this life where temptation will cease.

"Moral failure rarely happens with one sudden explosion;
it's normally a subtle erosion."
Larry Osborne

The good news is that there are things we can do to access God's strength. We can "strengthen our strengths" by doing what I call "praying ahead." By this I mean praying now about what may lie ahead. We not only have fault lines or weaknesses and times that we are more vulnerable and weak, but we also have times when we can sense the spiritual strength. "Lead us not into temptation." In THOSE times, in the strong times, we can pray a prayer like this: "Father, I know there will be times in the future when I am more weak or susceptible to temptation. When those moments happen, I ask You to remember this altar and this, my prayer right now, and empower me in that moment to walk in integrity. Though weak in THAT moment, let strength come from the prayer I pray to You in THIS moment. Lead me not into temptation in those moments, lead me out of them, or lead me through them."

As evidence of this woman's affections for Joseph grew, I can imagine him praying. Rather than waiting until the sudden onset of a "Pop Quiz" to cry out to God in desperation for help, he would have been cultivating that connection to the Lord so deeply ahead of time—looking to God ahead of time so much—that when the moment came it was natural to declare "How could I do such a wicked thing ... against God?"

Resisting temptation isn't just about being spiritually strong but it's also about being smart. In the moments when you are not strong you need to be smart. Stay out of the way! "Potiphar's wife is over here? Okay then I'll work over on the other side of the house." Avoid certain situations. The apostle Paul, lovingly told Timothy, his son in the faith, "flee youthful lusts." (2 Tim.2:22)

> **"It's really hard to fight what you are supposed to flee."**
>
> LARRY OSBORNE

In every person's life, there are "Fault Lines" (weaknesses) and we all have "Foundations" (bedrock strengths). Every decision I make strengthens one of the two. This applies to more than just sexual sin, but can apply to overeating, overspending, flying off in a fit of rage with your words, gossip, inappropriate work relationship, and much more. In your strong and sane moments, sabotage those opportunities. Disconnect the triggers that can cause a problem.

- Married friends, avoid intimate environments or conversations where unhealthy physical or emotional connections can develop between you and someone other than your spouse.

- Single friends, use wisdom in your dating relationships. Know what you need and be intentional with your boundaries. Don't set yourself up for temptation.
- Travel in hotels wisely. A mentor of mine would check into his room and unplug the TV.
- Get a filter on your internet.
- Use social media wisely. Limit what you look for. I know friends of mine who've gone on and said, "I'm going to go back into my past and look up this certain person." Listen, why do we need to go there? Social media can become the fertilizer for a problem.
- Discard the "I can handle this" mentality. Just because you handled a temptation once doesn't mean the next pop quiz won't result in a reaction that causes years of pain.

Jesus challenged His hearers to pluck their eyes out if their eyes caused them to stumble. I know a brother in Christ who deletes all games from his new computers or laptops because they are such time-wasting temptations for him. Whatever it takes! His friends and family have laughed at him and said "Really?" and he just smiles and is honest! "I can't get things accomplished with those on my computers."

When I was a youth pastor in Western NY, a situation happened as the teens were leaving after an event and a sudden lake effect snow rolled in. There was a girl whose parents couldn't come pick her up. It was one of several similar situations. I would literally call my wife Anna and put her on speakerphone as we drove. I recognized that there was a target on my back and so I intentionally brought my wife into the situation. Give the enemy no room. Be wise.

INTEGRITY CANNOT BE STOLEN, ONLY SAFEGUARDED OR SQUANDERED

Genesis 39:11–16 (author's comments in parentheses)
One day, however, no one else was around when he went in to do his work. She came and grabbed him by his cloak, demanding, "Come on,

sleep with me!" Joseph tore himself away, but he left his cloak in her hand as he ran from the house. When she saw that she was holding his cloak and he had fled, she called out to her servants (servants who were no doubt jealous of Joseph because of the favor put on him in Potiphar's house. Now she's rallying them to her cause). *Soon all the men came running. "Look!" she said. "My husband has brought this Hebrew slave here to make fools of us! He came into my room to rape me, but I screamed. When he heard me scream, he ran outside and got away, but he left his cloak behind with me."*

She kept the cloak with her until her husband came home. Then she told him her story. "That Hebrew slave you've brought into our house tried to come in and fool around with me," she said. (This blame game is as old as the first couple, Adam & Eve.) *"But when I screamed, he ran outside, leaving his cloak with me!"*

Joseph appeared to be a silent, submissive victim in every aspect of this narrative until that moment. This wife may have gotten Joseph's coat, but not his character.

Your integrity cannot be stolen from you. You are a steward of it. You can squander it, but nobody can take it. People can steal all kinds of things from you: your wallet, your car, your credit card, and your identity, but they cannot steal your integrity.

My integrity is mine to keep or mine to surrender. I can remember in high school being one of the first kids with a cell phone. Back then, cell phones were like bricks with huge antennas and awkward, but "Hey! I am the man! I have a cell phone!" I forgot my bag in study hall one day and then raced back to get it. There was that bag full of books, with all of my homework still there, but they took my cell phone. I was a victim; somebody took from me and I had no choice. I don't ever have to surrender my character, however. It's mine to lay down and mine to safeguard. These are decisions nobody can make for me.

God loves you so much and He loves the people He's called. He's gifted you to influence with so great a passion, that He wants to drill this into you as He did for Joseph. It is high on His list of desires for you. Become a winner and don't squander what God gave you.

> Genesis 39:19-20
> *Potiphar was furious when he heard his wife's story about how Joseph had treated her. So he took Joseph and threw him into the prison where the king's prisoners were held, and there he remained.*

"Winning within" is to always be in the center of God's will. There in the prison Joseph remained, having won within and won in the center of God's will, being trained for influence. Incidentally, because Potiphar was captain of the palace guard (think "secret police" or "executioners") Joseph could've been executed if Potiphar truly believed his wife's story. Seriously, you mess with the wife of the chief of police and imagine the consequences! What a testimony is being written however. Joseph won within that day, didn't surrender his integrity, and was in the perfect will of God.

Every decision you and I make will eventually become a story we tell. Without exception, when it comes to the pop quizzes that are life's temptations, and the opportunities we have to build the strong foundation or weaken the fault lines, each decision adds to a story. You may have to tell your story one day to an employer or to a jury or to your children and grandchildren. Ultimately one day we will stand before God, and even though He already knows the story, we will tell the story before Almighty God.

What kind of story do you want to tell your kids? Joseph would one day have a story to tell his two boys Ephraim and Manasseh. "Boys, your reputation is what people THINK you to be. Your character is what God KNOWS you to be. There is a big difference. It's never wrong to do the right thing. Even if you get in trouble for doing the right thing, protect the 'coat' of your integrity."

MY STORY

I recognize that this is a sobering subject and people can struggle with all kinds of condemnation over past indiscretions. So, I want to address this potential by being very honest about my past and my story. Part of my overcoming present temptation has had to deal with vulnerably facing my past.

I wish that I had the same story to tell that Joseph did, but I don't. As a youth pastor and pastor I am very passionate about this issue of sexual purity. I have helped thousands of youth, their families, and men grapple with these issues. I do not view pornography on the internet, but I am still a man. I experienced the same locker room talk others have on sports teams.

People have listened to my passion about this and said things like "Josh, you are the man!"

When those words are said, I remind myself I am a man, just a man.

Even though I grew up in a Godly home, and against the advice of my parents and leaders around me, I entered into a relationship with a non-Christian girl. It was a bad decision that started a chapter in my life story that I wish I didn't have to tell. Our mutual friends and the circle of friends she hung out with knew I was a Christian and encouraged her, "He's a good boy," and they teased me week after week to "go for it" with her.

Everything in my flesh wanted what this girl had, but everything in my spirit said, "Get out of there!" If I had only known that my wife Anna was just a few years around the corner. If I had only known the wife God had for me. If I had known that God has more for me than anyone else can give and that nobody else can take it away. But this other relationship went too serious, too deep, too quick, and I pushed beyond physical boundaries. I gave a gift to that person that was supposed to be preserved for my future wife. I relinquished my virginity in that situation. It was the worst decision I've ever made.

I thank God that the shame has been lifted and the old Josh is dead and not even alive anymore. I thank God that on October 21st of 2000, my life was significantly upgraded when I married the most amazing woman I've ever known. I don't deserve what I have.

Whatever the process or the story you have to tell, however good or imperfect it may be up to this point, God is able to teach you how to win within so that every decision you make from this point on, will tell a story that will positively impact future generations.

It's never wrong or too late to begin doing the right thing. The blood of Jesus cleanses you of all unrighteousness. His Word and not your past is the standard for your life right now. The strongest safeguard of your integrity is not a filter or an accountability partner, but a loving relationship with Jesus Christ. Cultivate that. God can help you forget things you should never remember, and remember things you should never forget.

"We should fear concealment more than confession."

PIERRE DUPLESSIS

07

KINGDOM COMMUNITY

There is a story of two steamboats that left Memphis about the same time, traveling down the Mississippi River to New Orleans. As they traveled side by side at about the same pace, they were neck and neck until one started pulling ahead of the other. Of course, men being men and sailors being sailors, those from one vessel started making a few remarks about the snail's pace of the other.

Words were exchanged as the trash talking continued. Challenges were made. The friendly talk turned into an all-out vicious competition as the two boats roared through the Deep South.

Then one boat began falling behind. Its issue was that it didn't have enough fuel. There had been plenty of coal for the trip, but not enough for a race. As the boat dropped back, an enterprising young sailor took some of the ship's cargo and tossed it into the ovens. When the sailors saw that the supplies burned as well as the coal, they fueled their boat with the material they had been assigned to transport. They ended up winning the race, but unfortunately, they burned their cargo.

With all of the dynamics that go into growing and developing an overcoming lifestyle, I just can't go on without devoting a chapter to the incredible importance of relationships in this walk of faith and victory. Community helps fuel our purity. We have to walk with Jesus for ourselves, but we can't walk with Jesus by ourselves.

God has entrusted precious cargo to us: children, spouses, friends, brothers and sisters in Christ. Our job is to do our part in not just seeing that we make it to our destination, but that our relational cargo remains intact and gets there with us. Life is not only about where we go or what we do, but who we become in the process and who we take with us along the way.

THE KING'S COMMUNITY TRAVELS TOGETHER

Anywhere worth going is worth going together. In fact, winning by yourself is losing. I am not in this battle by myself. You are not in this journey by yourself.

> "I have to follow Jesus Christ FOR myself,
> but I cannot follow Jesus BY myself."
> **Steven Furtick**

We receive care, connect, and grow spiritually as believers when we are in Kingdom community. It's a core value of walking out our faith. You can't do the "one anothers" in the New Testament (love one another, exhort one another, encourage one another, comfort one another, and so on) if we aren't walking with "others." Life in the Kingdom of God moves at the speed of relationships.

When you go on a trip in a vehicle, the first step is to make sure everyone gets in the car. And if we are going to make forward progress in our Christian life, we've got to open the doors of our heart and bring others along in our life journey. This requirement is for both our sakes and for theirs.

Being an overcomer has enough challenges without missing the key dynamic that we were created to do this life with others. We need their strength and they need ours. The greatest commodity in the church is people, not programs; it is people, rather than good preaching or beautiful new facilities.

Opening the door to more and deeper relationships in the church is risky business. "What if there are some weird people in that church or in those groups?"

Don't you worry at all about that; there WILL be. In fact, if you don't find at least one weird person in any small group or church, then it may be because you are the weird person in the group ("Not me!") and I want to encourage you to go mine the gold in those people around you anyway!

This is more significant than "joining a support group," and I love support groups and small groups. It's a mentality that embraces God's community of people for our own victory and for theirs. When striving to win within, when struggling to silence the voice of shame, when embracing the blessing of God's boundaries and escaping sin's slippery slope, it is easy to try to keep the issues "private" but it is absolutely essential that we resist the temptation to do this on our own.

Jackie Robinson was an amazing athlete. He eventually became a hall of fame baseball player. Yet, in his early days he struggled incredibly just to show up day-to-day at the stadium. Jackie was under intense pressure to perform as the first African American player in the big leagues. He was ridiculed, mocked, spit on, received threats against his family and worse. The movie 42 depicted a turning point that when later interviewed, Jackie would say it was one of the most influential moments of his life. Jackie had just made an error at first base. The stadium erupted with disgust and boos. Little did anyone know, besides Jackie, that he had reached his breaking point. This moment was the straw that was about to break the camel's back. Jackie couldn't take anymore. He was ready to cash it in when out of nowhere Pee Wee Reese, the team's shortstop, came over to stand next to Jackie. This was no small gesture. Reese was a ten-time all-star and widely respected throughout baseball. He was a leader on the team. His own family did not like the fact that he was playing with a man from the Negro league. Pee Wee didn't say anything to Jackie, he didn't have to, just his presence next to him, facing the booing mob and absorbing that moment with him was more than enough. Jackie turned a corner emotionally and decided to stick with it. Jackie and Pee Wee would never forget that moment, in fact, no one ever would due to an iconic statue of that moment being placed outside Coney Island's MCU park in Brooklyn, NY.

Don't miss the truth from this story: when we are surrounded, we are grounded.[15] Community helps make us immovable during tough times. This is why Jesus never commissioned His disciples to walk alone.

It is near impossible to knock over a Sequoia Redwood Tree. Know why? It's not just because they are massive. It's also not because they have the deepest roots. It's because their root systems not only go down but they also grow out. Redwood trees don't grow alone, they always grow in groves. This is because they rely on the stability of intertwining their root systems together with the other *giants* around them. That just may be the word you needed. Surround yourself with some giants. Find some people with deep roots and begin to do life with them. When we are surrounded we become grounded.

A COMMUNITY BUILT ON SINCERE LOVE

The Apostle Paul was a "master builder" in the New Testament church. In fact, in Romans 12 he gave a blueprint for the church community, a reminder that we are built into a household of faith, joined as a body of believers, and born into a family of sons and daughters. For purposes of this chapter in *Overcome*, I'm going to focus on the one building block Paul emphasized the most, "Sincere Love."

Romans 12:9 (NIV)
Love must be sincere. Hate what is evil; cling to what is good.

What is "sincere" love? How is this so vital for the one who intends to apprehend the overcoming life? How is it a foundational building block for relationship?

The word "sincere" means "without mixture or pretending." You can't try to love people and try to impress people at the same time. When you've got hidden secrets and you don't want to humble yourself and ask for help or prayer or accountability, you will then be tempted to overcompensate for the insecure feelings inside by trying to impress people. It's false and anything but sincere.

> **"No love is conditional. If love is conditional, it's just some sort of manipulation masquerading as love."**
>
> DONALD MILLER[17]

Biblical love cannot be earned by impressing someone. Love can only be given. Impressing people is not love. To fulfill the destiny God has created you for and for which He is training you, you're going to have to lay down your pride and connect through hard relational work including loving confrontation.

It's impossible to love people that you're trying to impress. In fact, the loneliest people on the planet are those who are trying to con others. How can you bond with people that you're trying to manipulate?

You can't earn love anyway; it can only be given. So, you can't earn love by "having your life together" or by appearing a certain way or by living at a certain level of sinless-ness. Love is your choice to give or the choice of others to give to you. Trying to impress only cuts off the possibility of either.

"THE TUNNEL OF CHAOS"[16]

There are different levels of community that a believer needs to push through, or be open to, in order to experience the kind of Biblical Kingdom Community that strengthens us the way God intends.

On one level are the people who are just "around". You interact with them as acquaintances, but there's no deep connection. You might call it "Acquaintance Community." In-a-nutshell conversations at this level of community go something like this:

"How are you?"
"Good. You?"
"Good."
"Well, praise the Lord, good then. We're all good."

Now there's a place for this level of relationship, even a need for that in daily life. Yes, we share the highlights of our life, whether in person, tweeting, or on Instagram. We don't share everything with everybody, though. Your valley moments in life are not going to be shared with everybody in this crowd.

Every inner circle friendship, every marriage, every relationship starts in that broader community. You meet there. Do you want more? That is the question, that if answered as a "yes" opens the door to a higher level of community and relationship.

What we really long for down deep is an "Authentic Community." This level of connection is where the masks come down, where there is no façade, and where I'm not trying to manipulate you, or vice versa. This place is where love can be given and doesn't have to be earned (not that it's even possible for true love to be earned.) At this level of community, across the table and face-to-face, a conversation can progress to "Well, how are you … really?" to which a reply might be "I'm struggling with …" This is where people get real. This is where help comes from in the Kingdom of God.

There's just one small "catch." To get from the Acquaintance Community to the Authentic Community more representative of the Kingdom of God and sincere love, you must travel through this tunnel that Bill Hybels coined the phrase "The Tunnel of Chaos."

"The Tunnel of Chaos" is as pleasant as its name! Yet if your goal is take other precious cargo to victory, and for it to carry you to victory … if your goal is to get back up from the slope of sin or out of the swamp of shame, there's no other way than to surrender to the path that leads through this tunnel to Authentic Kingdom Community. Every close relationship started in the Acquaintance crowd with a "hello" but it can't become close without going through the process of this tunnel.

How do you open the door to this tunnel of chaos, to get from acquaintance and artificial to authentic? There are two keys to open the door. The first is confession and the other is confrontation.

CONFESSION

Opening the door to Authentic Kingdom Community requires some intentionality. A confession might be "I'm struggling with this." Or it could be "You thought I was this, but I'm really that." I John says not to be afraid of sincerity and openness because confession and walking in the light actually brings greater bonding and deeper levels of relationship.

You are probably not going to go out into the lobby after church and begin to share your deep, dark secrets. It wouldn't even be wise. There is a place for the larger crowd and the acquaintances, and there's a need for the "around the table" interactions where that kind of confession can take place.

Jesus Himself modeled this beautifully. He was sinless, but He was NOT struggle-free. By the time He was in the Garden of Gethsemane, He had gone from the crowd of disciples, to the twelve, and then took just three, Peter, James and John with Him further into the Garden. To those three He said, "My soul is deeply troubled." He confessed that He was burdened with grief. Sweat like drops of blood poured from His brow. This confession was a model of incredible vulnerability. "We're about to bond deeper right now."

CONFRONTATION

The second key is confrontation. The word "confrontation" is scary to most of us, but Biblical confrontation is not a tool we use to put someone down. It's an action which is intended to preserve the relationships that are going to mutually strengthen one another for the journey ahead. We don't confront someone Biblically if we're just trying to prove that we're right and the other is wrong. God didn't mean for us to want to win arguments.

We need people in our lives who love us enough to correct us! In the very next breath, after Paul said, "let your love be sincere" (without mixture), he said "Hate what is evil; cling to what is good." When I love you sincerely and without mixture, then I also have earned the right to hate what is evil in your life. The people who love me the most are those who hate what is evil in me. Confronters aren't trying to impress you or get something from you, but they love you enough to tell you like it is. Now there are some who claim to "tell it like it is" about their own life, saying "I'm not ashamed; this is just what I think." when what they are really saying is "I'm in sin and I don't care what you or anybody thinks about it."

That's NOT what we're talking about here.

We're talking about a connection of confession and confrontation, the goal of which is greater faith, joy and victory in life. We have to do this with some people, but we can't with everyone. So, what's the process? It means surrendering our heart to this tunnel of awkward, difficult, sometimes painful, but honest, conversations. The ones that open the door to authentic, deeper relationship.

WHAT AVOIDING THE TUNNEL LOOKS LIKE

Jesus also modeled for us that in relationships you never lower the boundaries or your values and standards in order to let people into your life. There was a rich, young ruler whom Jesus WANTED to follow Him. He WANTED Him to come into authentic, deeper relationship. Jesus INVITED the young man to leave the artificial community of acquaintances at the crowd level and come to the table of deep fellowship with the Son of God, the Messiah.

The young man's journey through the tunnel of chaos was unsuccessful because of a confrontation that he would not embrace. The trip went something like this: "I see something in your heart that is holding you back from authentic relationship with Me as a disciple. Here's what you need to do to go further in this: sell all you have, give it to the poor, and then follow Me."

"Uhh,…No. No way."

The relationship went no deeper.

The Bible says that Jesus was "sorrowful." Jesus was not willing to drag the rich, young ruler through the tunnel from one level of relationship to another by lowering the standards for getting there. He wouldn't force the man to the table. The rich young ruler had an image; at one level, relationships can be all about "image." At the table of authenticity, it's all about "intimacy," and Jesus was sorrowful that the young man would not use the necessary keys to open the door to intimacy.

I wanted to take one chapter and dedicate it to these Kingdom connections of relationship because there's so much fear directed at this process of getting beyond the image, at this process I call a tunnel.

People think "If others see the way I really am and if they know what I really struggle with, they will run away," but the Bible says "Actually, we have better fellowship together when we walk in the light."

In *Scary Close*, Donald Miller added: "We don't think of our flaws as the glue that binds us to the people we love, but they are. Grace only sticks to our imperfections. Otherwise you don't need grace."

If we play it safe, we rob the world of what God is doing in our lives and of who God has made us to be. Your Father created you for a destiny that you are intended to live out with and for other people; don't keep them from that. Get to the end of the journey together with others.

Romans 12:10
Be devoted to one another in brotherly love.

There was an image for HBO's *Band of Brothers* with a tagline that said, "They depended on one another because the world depended on them." The local church is the hope of the world. Or there's *The Lord of the Rings* series where Frodo says "Go back, Sam. I'm going to Mordor alone!" Sam replied, "Of course you are. And I'm coming with you!"

I'm so glad that there are some friends who don't care if you or I are going through hell; their attitude is that "You're not going through hell alone." You don't find friends like that in the Acquaintance Community, in the crowd. You might meet them there, but you don't find out if they are that kind of friend until you open your heart to the tunnel process that puts you across the table in a lifestyle of confession and confrontation.

WHAT IT LOOKS LIKE INSIDE THE TUNNEL

So, if the process from Acquaintance Community to Authentic Community goes through this Tunnel, how does that work? What is it really like walking day to day through that tunnel into the realm of deeper relationship with people who can travel towards a destination carrying each other? I think the process includes some very natural stages, as we keep saying "Yes" to the Lord and reject the fear of vulnerability.

Stage 1 | Convenience
This level says "I'm here among these people because it's easy. It's convenient." Maybe I like the church, or the event, or the programs, or the atmosphere, or the activity, or the mission. Many other people are here, but what initially drew us here was some shared convenience or interest.

Stage 2 | Connection
At some point through the tunnel of relationship building, there is a maturing that happens so that I'm not just there because of convenience, but

because of connection. "I'm here because I'm connected to people, certain people, people who are here with me."

Stage 3 | Conviction

Further down the path through the tunnel, relationships mature beyond convenience and connection, to conviction. At this level of relationship, I'm saying "There are some things here in this or these relationships that I like and some things I don't like, things that match my preferences and some that don't. I'm here because I'm called to be here. I'm with this person because I'm called to stay loyal to this person. Offenses may come, but we'll work through them."

"I CAN'T"

Some might say "Hey, I'm not very good at this community stuff. Paul said in Rom 9:13 "Practice." Saying "I can't do community" is to deny the fact that God created you with the ability to connect with people in a life-giving way. You were created to walk, but you didn't do it right out of the birth canal; you had to "practice." Try reaching out. Try lending a hand. Try connecting with a new person and asking them about themselves. Try giving a word of encouragement. Try participating in small group venues that are a stretch of faith. Practice, practice and practice and add your prayers to that, asking God "Who can I pour into?" Ask Him for friends and people with whom you can walk this road to victory and Godly destiny.

There's no way around this next fact: Seeking to develop a sense of community in your life for your own spiritual and moral well-being is extremely costly. Once you've experienced healthy, life-giving, "doing life together" kinds of relationships, you'll pay the price, whatever it is, to continue having them.

My hot water tank in my house went out recently. Now I recognize that this is not on the list of the world's greatest problems, so maybe that makes me, and many of you, spoiled. But when you grow up and live in a culture that always has hot water for hot showers, have you ever gone without? When I return home from a mission trip, I'm thankful for my family, and I'm thankful for a hot shower! This new water heater cost me about twice what I had expected, but when you have gotten accustomed to hot showers, you will pay whatever it takes to get hot water back.

The life-strengthening benefits of Kingdom Community relationships are that same way. They will cost you more than you estimate, but they are worth whatever price you have to pay. There will be time spent that you could have used on other things. There will be patience required, opportunities for offense, disappointment, and pain. I have to be honest: when you do community right, it hurts! Some of those you bond with will have changes in life that come along and take them away from you; others will pass away. That hurts. The price is real, but it's worth it. It's part of what Jesus died for. God Himself paid the biggest price, so that flawed human beings like you and I could experience Kingdom Community.

> John 11:44
> *The dead man (Lazarus) came out, his hands and feet wrapped with strips of linen, and a cloth around his face. Jesus said to them, "Take off the grave clothes and let him go."*

Lazarus needed help to walk out the resurrection life he was given; so do we. Resurrection power from God is unpacked in restorative community. God's people help up us unpack and continue to live in God's power.

Take the attitude that says, "We're going to write this story together." There's a story that lives inside of you. Have you created an environment where you can share that story? As you are vulnerable and give of your faith, love and humility, God will give back to you relational fulfillment at a whole new level. Your story, your encouragement, your challenge, your life … may be exactly what carries some extra and precious human cargo to their God-given destination.

"You were born to think like a man... but you've been born again to think like God."

***

JOSHUA FINLEY

08

THE TRUTH ABOUT YOU

Upgrades in life are great! Nothing puts a smile on a face quicker than finding out at the last moment that your airline seat has been upgraded from Economy to First Class! Honestly though, most upgrades are luxuries and certainly not necessities. In fact, the job of most sales people is to "help" you think and feel like upgrades are a "necessity" so that you'll pay a little more of your money and buy the upgrade. It could be the next higher class in a rental car, the upgrade to your internet service, or a premium phone plan.

I'm sure I frustrate a lot of sales people because I do enough research ahead of time to know what I want before I go in to make the purchase, and I'm not going to be convinced by a sales pitch. If they want to give me the upgrade for free I'll take it, but otherwise, "Give me what I came for and let's move on."

The best upgrades in life are the ones you desperately need and someone else pays for. When Anna and I were engaged and planning our marriage, one of the things we hadn't really counted was the cost of all of the furniture we would need to have for our apartment as a couple. Neither of our twin beds were going to do. The twin bed that I had since about age seven was disintegrating and hardly suitable for one adult person much less a couple. Thankfully, even though we hadn't counted on this cost of marriage ahead of time, our parents all chipped in and bought us a brand-new bed. What a blessing! That was not a luxury but a genuine need, and someone else paid for it.

Salvation is the most essential upgrade in this life and the life to come. It's one you must have, and Jesus paid for it before you even knew that you needed it.

WHAT YOU BELIEVE IS TRUE ABOUT YOU MATTERS

In the area of overcoming sin, I love feeling good and I love it when I feel victorious but to live a victorious Christian life there comes a point when it has to go beyond your feelings. There has to be a knowing. In the struggle with sin and temptation there will always be peaks and valleys, highs and lows, but when we're in the valleys, we need a knowing or a conviction that lifts us above and beyond our feelings in those moments.

Sometimes people shy away from "theology" (the word simply means "study of God") but I like to think of it this way. We can add theology to the framework of our life on the mountain tops that will grab hold of us when our feelings are in the valleys, and lift us back out.

Another way of looking at it is like this: every human being has a skeletal bone structure that holds up our bodies. Each of us look different, act different, have different talents and I.Q.'s, but without a skeleton none of us would function very well. It's the framework upon which a body, with its unique appearances, can be built.

Every believer in Christ will look different, have different and unique callings, gifting, and life purposes but the truth of God is what makes the "skeleton." It's the Truth of God that gives us all strength and a framework upon which God can build a victorious and purposeful life that goes the distance.

2 Corinthians 5:17 (NKJV)

Therefore, if anyone is in Christ, he is a new creation; old things have passed away; behold, all things have become new.

What does it mean to be a new creation?

When I was first driving at age 16, being one of six kids, there was no way I was going to be driving anything very nice. I drove a 5-speed, beat up 1987 Chevy Nova that I called "White Lightning." It didn't start well, so I usually parked it on a hill so that if and when I needed to, I could "pop the clutch" in order to start the engine. If hills were not available to park on for the next startup, White Lightning was small enough that I could put her in neutral, open the door, push it forward, get it rolling and then jump in and pop the clutch to crank the engine and get it started.

Eventually, an upgrade was needed so I bought a 1992 Acura Integra. Not only was it newer in *time* (from an '87 to a '92), but it was newer in *kind* (from a Chevy to an Acura).

Salvation isn't just a matter of God cleaning you up and dusting you off, re-painting, and having you make some holy New Year's Resolutions, as in "I'm going to turn over a new leaf now." God isn't saying "I want to just make a better version of you." When you put your faith in Christ as Savior, you were made new in time and new in kind.

When it says, "Old things have passed away," obviously your body didn't pass away, but the old you did. Like a worn-out Nova getting sent to the junkyard, the old you got buried with Jesus in the grave and in Christ, a new you was born.

In fact, after receiving salvation the temptation is to try to "clean up your life" in your own strength and by your own will power. You'll hear people who came to Christ and with a past of struggling with severe substance abuse say things like "I'm just going to have to surrender more sincerely, try harder, get more serious about it." Getting serious is important, but Paul addressed the

Galatians about this tendency to try to clean up our lives by our own works when he asked them in essence, "So, did you get saved by your faith or by your good works? It was by faith! So, having begun in the Spirit are you going to try to keep moving forward by your own good works and will power?"[18]

It doesn't work. Salvation is not a goal to be achieved but a gift to be received. You are not a better and sweeter version of yourself. God has made you a completely new person.

THE TRUTH ABOUT WHAT HAPPENED WHEN I BELIEVED

> Romans 10:13
> *For "Everyone who calls on the name of the Lord will be saved."*

What does it mean to be "saved?" How amazing is what happens to you? The Greek word "Sozo" which is translated "saved," literally means all of the following by definition:

- To save, to keep safe and sound
- To rescue from danger or destruction
- To save a suffering one from perishing
- To preserve one who is in danger of destruction
- To deliver from the penalties of the judgment
- To make one whole in spirit, soul, and body

All of that is the upgrade you were given when you were "saved." That incredible upgrade is one you didn't have to pay or work for.

THE UPGRADED LIFE YOU WERE GIVEN IS ETERNAL

> Romans 6:23
> *For the wages of sin is death, but the free gift of God is eternal life through Christ Jesus our Lord.*

1 John 5:13

I have written this to you who believe in the name of the Son of God, so that you may know you have eternal life.

There's no reason for you to be living with any sense of "eternal insecurity," and there's no need to wonder if you got saved or really saved, or "Do I need to get saved again?" Paul and John agree that it's possible to KNOW that you have eternal life. If I gave you a Christmas gift, you don't wonder whether or not you have it; the only question is whether you open it and receive it. Did you embrace with humility the fact that you can't earn eternal salvation, acknowledge your sin and your need to be saved, and receive salvation from God?

Salvation makes new your past, present and future. Of course, we all easily understand that salvation means a new eternal future in heaven. It is the "past-ness" of salvation that is so critical to help us overcome present sin battles.

Past	Present	Future[19]
God was	God is	He is to come
Have been saved	Are being saved	Will be saved
Spirit was saved	Soul is being saved	Body will be new
From the penalty of sin	From the power of sin	From the presence of sin

BELIEVE THE PAST TO ENJOY THE PRESENT

It is so critical to believe what is true about the past tense of salvation, in order to enjoy the present process of winning within and becoming an overcomer. Understanding what Christ has already done will produce peace in the present circumstances and faith as we look to the future. If you don't understand

and believe what He's already done, then you'll live like a person who doesn't have that, and you'll live under pressure in the present and in fear or worry towards the future.

Another reason it's critical to believe what is true about the past tense of salvation is that "Believing is seeing" or in other words, believing that Christ has already made you a new person unlocks the grace to overcome sin in the present.

Too often we want to be like Thomas and say, "Seeing is believing," or "When I SEE that I have the victory over sin, then I'll believe it." In actuality, believing FIRST that Christ put the old you to death and made you new is key to seeing it come to pass experientially.

WHAT DID JESUS DEPOSIT IN YOUR SPIRITUAL BANK ACCOUNT?

Look at the many references to what Christ has done for us and how God looks at us after we come to Christ. Notice all of the words that are in the past tense: approved, saved, beloved, justified, redeemed, loved, and accepted just to name a few, plus my favorite one: "It is finished."

If I went to the bank where you have an account and made a deposit in your account, what would be the impact? That depends on how much I deposited and what you believe? For instance, if you have $300 in a savings account and that's all you have to your name, and I go in and make a deposit of $1,000,000, how much do you now have? Well, you now would have a million dollars plus three hundred dollars, of course.

What if you don't believe that I did it, however? What if you don't write it in your bank book and refuse to believe that I really did that? Then you would continue to live like a person with $300 to your name. If you believed me then you would begin living like a millionaire.

There are a lot of people struggling with sin in the present tense because they don't believe that Jesus Christ already put their old nature to death on the cross. Here's the truth that we have to embrace:

Romans 6:11 (NKJV)
Likewise you also, reckon yourselves to be dead indeed to sin, but alive to God in Christ Jesus our Lord.

"Reckon" is a mathematical term—a banking term. Here's how it works. Have you ever played the board game *The Game of LIFE*? You drive this car around the board, get paydays, buy insurances, get married, have kids, play the Stock Market, and do all kinds of "life" things until late in the game you drive into a space that says, "Day of Reckoning." There you cash in your assets and find out just how much your net worth is.

Paul is saying that God has made a deposit in your spiritual bank account which says, "this person is dead to sin." The old you, that is, is dead, and you are a new creature.

What if you don't believe that God did that, however? If you don't believe that truth, then you'll believe lies and say things like "Well, I'm Irish and I just have an anger problem" or "I have a pride problem" or "I'm a worrier" or "I have a lust issue."

In reality, according to the Bible, the new you does NOT have any of those issues. The OLD you did, but the old you was "crucified with Christ" according to Galatians. More accurately, the TRUTH is that "the old me was a worrier and the old me had an anger problem but that is not the new me and God is helping me break free of the patterns that the old me walked in." Neither I nor the Apostle Paul are playing mental gymnastics with you. This isn't "mind over matter." It's not making excuses ("Not my fault! The devil made me do it.") No. This is a matter of believing what is the truth about you and the truth about the spiritual deposit that the living resurrected God has made in your spiritual bank account.

Believe! Believe that you are a new creature! "I am a new creature in Christ.

Old things have passed away. Old identities have passed away! My old nature and desires and alliances with lies have passed away. My spirit has been made new. I have new desires, new tendencies, and a whole new nature. I am NOT a slave to sin, but I'm dead to sin. It's in my account."

THE LAWS OF SIN AND GRAVITY

Paul said it later in Romans as he described his own battles with sin:

Romans 7:17 (NKJV)
So now, it is no longer I who do it, but sin that dwells in me.

Paul said in Romans 7:15, "I do not understand what I do. For what I want to do - I do not do, but what I hate—I do."

We've all been there, right?

You determine to quit some disappointing habit or pattern that has hurt you and your loved ones. You convince yourself that this time you messed up for the last time (down deep you may know better). You steel yourself up; you're determined.

As sincere as you are about that determination and resolve, soon your new-found sincerity to do better is tested. BOOM! You failed!

This is what I call the "I Blew It Again" problem. Haven't you been there with me? Feeling lower than a snake's belly, guilty and ashamed, you come crawling back to the Lord: "Oh, God, I'm so sorry. I blew it again. I meant it when I said I loved you. I don't know why I did it. I don't ever want to do that again, I promise I'll do better, with YOUR HELP of course…" And then we start all over again.

Again and again we continue the patterns of praying, trying, failing, feeling ashamed, losing confidence in our standing with God. Doubts and guilt constantly nag. This impedes the very confidence God wants us to have before

His throne.

In verse 23 of that chapter, Paul talked about "the law of sin at work" within his members. "The Law of Sin"? I like to think of it like the law of gravity in the world of physics. If you throw a brick up in the air above your head, the law of gravity will bring it painfully down. People have varying levels of willpower for their resolutions, but if you try to fight the law of sin with your fleshly efforts, eventually in some areas of your life, you'll lose.

The good news is that both in the natural and in the spiritual there are superseding laws. In physics gravity always wins … UNLESS, you supersede that law by putting into effect the "laws of aerodynamics" by which megatons of steel can fly through the air loaded with people going from one airport to another.

We can't live under the law of sin and win, so why not supersede it with something more powerful? Paul found it and so can you! He called it "The Law of the Spirit of Life in Christ Jesus."

> Romans 8:2-3 (NKJV) author's comments in parentheses, underlining added
> *For the law of the Spirit of life in Christ Jesus <u>has made me</u>* (PAST TENSE) *free from the law of sin and death. For what the law could not do in that it was weak through the flesh, God did by sending His own Son in the likeness of sinful flesh, on account of sin: He condemned sin in the flesh.*

How do we operate in that superseding law? Again, the key is knowing, believing and identifying with the truth! Identify yourself with Christ who defeated that law of sin, and begin operating in this law of the Spirit of life.

In Colossians 1:27 Paul declared a powerful mystery that had been hidden from the prophets and all people until our day, this day of the Christian church, and that glorious powerful mystery, Paul said, is "Christ in you, the hope of glory." The new law of the Spirit is found through faith in Jesus Christ, who now has come to live inside of you. Whatever you used to think of yourself, you are now a carrier of the Presence of Christ.

Faith in your new identity is important. When I start recognizing which "person" has the "issues" (the old me or the new me), I recognize that it's the old me that fell or falls into sin. I stop taking ownership of the issue (lust, anger, gambling, or addiction) as my personal identity and I then can see myself as God does, through His Son. The more I BELIEVE and SEE myself the way He does, in light of the truth of God, the more I'll BECOME that way. Believing (the truth) is seeing (the manifestation).

WHAT OLD THINGS PASSED AWAY?

> Colossians 2:11-15 (NLT) author's comments added
> *When you came to Christ, you were "circumcised," but not by a physical procedure. Christ performed a spiritual circumcision—the cutting away of your sinful nature.*

What Christ cut away was the propensity to sin.

> *For you were buried with Christ when you were baptized. And with him you were raised to new life because you trusted the mighty power of God, who raised Christ from the dead. You were dead because of your sins and because your sinful nature was not yet cut away.*

"Not yet cut away" is the operative phrase there, and notice all the past tenses again. Because of Christ however, that propensity is no more.

> *Then God made you alive with Christ, for he forgave all our sins. He canceled the record of the charges against us and took it away by nailing it to the cross.*

The son of a farmer once asked, "Dad, sometimes I don't feel like I'm saved. How do I know that I'm really a Christian and saved?"

His dad said "Son, do you see how those pigs love to find the mud hole and go wallow in it? It's because by nature they love to get muddy. Now put sheep in that same pen, and they may accidentally stumble into some mud and get dirty once in a while, but they don't WANT to go there. That's how it is when you get saved. Sinners don't mind sinning and often want to. Once you're saved, you don't WANT to go there anymore."

Before Christ, you had a nature that dominated who you were, the sin nature. Christ put it to death.

YOU BOUGHT A STEERING WHEEL?

Salvation is so much more than forgiveness; let's look at all Jesus truly did for us!

Saying that Christ forgave you is true, but it's like buying a new car as an upgrade and going to your friend and telling him that you bought a new steering wheel. Yes that is true you did get a new steering wheel, but that is only a small part of the story. When Christ forgave our sins, that was only a part of the story. He put the old you to death and gave you a whole new nature.

You've heard people, when they've had a serious rift develop between them and a relative, say something like "That person is dead to me. I'm not talking to them anymore. I'm having nothing to do with them."

Biblically, you are dead to yourself! As Bill Johnson says, "Jesus didn't just die *for* you, but He also died *as* you." He did this so that He could resurrect a new you. The old you is dead to the new you, and you don't have to talk to the old you or talk like the old you or have anything to do with the old you anymore. "Reckon it dead" to you.

> **"Jesus didn't just die for you, He died as you."**
>
> BILL JOHNSON

Your legal status changed. You didn't just get forgiven, but you got a whole upgrade! There was a day that we sinned because we had to. Now in Christ, when we sin, it's because we choose to. In Romans 6:5-11 Paul made it clear that you are no longer a slave to sin and that sin no longer has power or dominion over you. Why believe or live like a slave when you're not one anymore?

THE TRUTH ABOUT WHY I STILL STRUGGLE WITH SIN?

If Christ did all of this for us, and my old nature was crucified in Christ, why do I still struggle with sin? Great question! There are still three major things working against us: the world, our flesh, and the devil.

The World

It seems clear both from Scripture and from observation that the gap between the wickedness of the world and the righteousness of the Church is going to get wider and wider. We live in a fallen world.

Revelation 22:11 (NLT) says it this way:

> *Let the one who is doing harm continue to do harm; let the one who is vile continue to be vile; let the one who is righteous continue to live righteously; let the one who is holy continue to be holy.*

The bad news and depravity of the world keeps getting worse and worse, but over the broad course of history around the world, the church in the nations keeps getting stronger and stronger. Despite how things may seem culturally and politically in the United States, even here I wouldn't trade the condition of the Christian Church now for what it was in 1957. God is building His Kingdom in lives. He isn't fretting over the bad news, and we ought not to doubt the power of God to transform a life no matter how wide the gap is. There are no lost causes for the power of God. Billy Graham said, "It's the Holy Spirit's job to convict, it's God's job to judge, and it's my job to love."

I saw this Tweet from Ray Ortlund that I loved,

"The apostles weren't wringing their hands saying,

'What's this world coming to?' They were exclaiming, 'Look what's come to the world!'"

Heaven is our destination, but our assignment is bringing more of heaven to bear upon earth! The more we realize who Christ has made us to be as His Church and Bride, the less we'll be looking for a rescue out of this world and the more love and truth we'll be sharing.

Your Flesh

As a new creation in Christ you don't have a sinful nature anymore, but you live in a body, and you have a flesh. Your flesh has an appetite for sin, so when opportunities arise to sin, your flesh always votes "yes." Your spirit man is connected to God, perfectly righteous, redeemed and accepted, and is always going to vote "no."

The battle is not with a sinful old nature, because that was done away with. Our battle is with flesh and this is an important distinction. Jesus dealt with the sinful nature, but we must deal with the flesh; the good news is that we know how to deal with it! You don't battle flesh with flesh.

A few years ago I bought a new iPhone, but I liked the size of the old one. For this reason, I bought the SE version, where they put the new operating system in the old case or framework. It was the old, smaller case, but a new operating system. In the same way, God gave you a new spirit, but He put that new spirit in an old body, an old carrying case if you will.

Why did He do that? Because God said, "I'll give 'em a new glorified body soon, but in the meantime, I've got work for them to do here on this earth, and I'm confident that the new power of the resurrected Son inside of them will be enough for them to win victoriously over the power of the flesh. My grace is more powerful than sin."

Our mind, renewed by the Word of God, is the veto power vote, deciding, "Am I going with my flesh or am I going with my spirit?"

Our flesh has appetites. Try fasting to see your fleshly appetites rear their ugly heads. The flesh can crave TV or video games, can envy, lust, or covet. The fight for us as Christians is between our inner man and our outer man. You don't have two natures crammed into your Spirit. Before you were a believer you were controlled by sin in your spirit and in your flesh (it was a unified rebellion). Now that you are a new creation, you have a new spirit and new nature in an old body. Therein lies the war within your members.

You can't become a conqueror in this war without a challenge. It reminds me of Old Testament Israel when they came out of the wilderness. They crossed the River Jordan with a promise from God that this land was theirs to own. Initially, many of their victories came so easily (think Jericho, march around, blow some trumpets, give a shout, and watch the fortress fall down before you). The victories came easy for a while but then as they moved forward further, the resistance was stronger and the battles for ground became more difficult. The Bible says that God wanted the young men to become conquerors. God wants you to become a conqueror. When you get saved, some sin battles fall away quickly. Others don't seem to go away so easily, but "Thanks be to God who always leads us in His triumph."[20]

The Devil

To the question of why you still struggle with sin, I'll give the least attention to the third contributor. The devil is not as powerful as you think he is. He's a defeated foe.

Remember the *The Wizard of Oz*? How frightened we all were by the Wizard, that is, until he was exposed. The smoke and mirrors and amplified voice made him sound more hideous than he was. Isaiah 14:15-16 says of Satan that he'll be brought down one day and people will see him on the last day and say, "Is *this* the one who made the nations tremble?"

I'm not saying that the devil isn't wreaking havoc or tormenting people and causing harm. My point is that in your battle against sin, he's less of a threat to you than your fleshly appetites.

Bob Mumford used to tell a story of Satan sitting on a curb outside of church with his head in his hands, all distraught. Someone asked, "What's wrong with you, Satan?" to which he answered, "These people! They keep blaming me for stuff I've never even done!"

THREE THINGS WORKING FOR YOU

Yes, you have the world, your flesh, and the devil working against you, but you've got three powerful things working *for* you, and it's not even a "fair fight." If this was a basketball game, it would be the worst "3-on-3" match up of all time.

> Romans 8:31
> *If God is for you, who can be against you?*

You have the Spirit of God, the Word of God, and the people of God working for you. Jesus sent out His followers "like sheep among wolves."[21] How can Jesus do something that sounds so risky? He could do it because He gave the disciples these three allies—allies that allowed them to go with the confidence that they had all the power and authority they needed.

I won't spend time on the "people of God" here, because all of Chapter Six was devoted to Kingdom community, but let's look at the other two.

The Spirit of God

The virus of sin was so bad that God gave us a whole new operating system. God the Father sent Jesus the Son to kill off your old nature. Then Jesus sent God the Holy Spirit to release in you the power of this divine new nature.

He has made His divine power available to us!

I remember how excited we'd be on Christmas to open gifts that my parents had bought us. I'd rip off the paper and be so happy to see what was inside! I also knew I didn't deserve it, so it was that much more incredible! Then

I'd read those dreaded words: "Batteries Not Included." What? No power? What's a gift with no power to operate it? Then mom would smile and reach back behind her and pull out a 24-pack of new batteries because she had the foresight to know that we needed power.

God had the foresight to know that you needed His power, and He's put it inside you. Plug into God's power. Ask Him to fill you with the Holy Spirit in a fresh way. "Seek earnestly the spiritual gifts,"[22] Paul said to the Corinthians. Don't consider the gifts as options. Some people look at the gifts of the Holy Spirit like they are some option to Christian living. Do you want to tell God "No Thanks" for His gifts? Yes, I know that His gifts are for power in evangelism and for ministering to others, but Paul also said that the gifts of the Holy Spirit are important for building ourselves up inside. Do we need being built up inside for this war or not? Then we need all the gifts of the Holy Spirit. They are tools to build with and weapons to fight with not toys to play with.

> Romans 8:6 (NIV)
> *The mind governed by the flesh is death, but the mind governed by the Spirit is life and peace.*

> Romans 5:12 (NIV)
> *Therefore, brothers and sisters, we have an obligation— but it is not to the flesh, to live according to it.*

God has given you a new Spirit and a new mind. You have no obligation to sin any longer because the Holy Spirit supernaturally removes any and all obligation you ever had to the flesh in the past!

The Word of God
What are you preaching to yourself?

It has been said, "Be careful what you say to yourself because you are always listening!" Your mind is the biggest battleground. It may be easier to not sin in church while the preacher is preaching but the truth is this: *You preach more messages to yourself than anyone else does, because you are always with yourself.*

Jesus defeated temptation the same way we must, not with human willpower, but with the truth. The "renewed mind," which is the thought-life washed by the truth of God's Word, is that which reminds me of what Christ did and empowers me to live accordingly. The enemy comes and plants thoughts attacking your mind. His thoughts are always lies, all of them. Is your mind renewed with the Word enough to veto the lies and carry you over the bridge to victory? If not, we find ourselves trying to resist sin in our own willpower, and it's all about our willpower and our trying harder.

> **The Bible is an all-you-can-eat buffet, but it's self-serve.**

The words of God (the Bible, on paper) are the thoughts of God spoken by the Holy Spirit. His Words renew my mind so that I can keep connecting to Him and to the truth about what He's already done, and who He's made me to be. The mind renewed by the truth keeps me linked to my new nature. Sin keeps trying to pull me, in my mind, back to my old nature.

Isaiah 43:18 (NKJV) author's comment in parentheses
"Do not remember the former things, nor consider the things of old (there's a new way to live).

Romans 12:2 (author's underlining added)
Don't copy the behavior and customs of this world, <u>but let God</u> transform you into a new person by changing the way you think.

That Greek word which is translated into "transform" is the word from which we also get "metamorphosis." It describes the process by which a caterpillar is changed into a different form. Just when the caterpillar thinks the world is over, it becomes a butterfly.

How does this renewing of the mind take place? I can't control every thought that ENTERS my mind but I can certainly control how I ENGAGE with those thoughts.

You are the most predictable preacher you will ever listen to, every day, all day, incessantly. Even while I'm preaching and listeners are listening, they are also listening to themselves. You don't like the way you are preaching to yourself? Then change the way you think. You change the way you think by letting your mind be renewed by the Word of truth.

Why am I emphasizing the mind so much? Because of what God knows about the human mind!

> Ephesians 4:17-21 (author's underlining added)
> *With the Lord's authority, I say this: Live no longer as the Gentiles do, for they are <u>hopelessly confused.</u> Their <u>minds</u> are full of darkness; they wander far from the life God gives because they have closed their <u>minds</u> and hardened their hearts against him. They have no sense of shame. They live for lustful pleasure and eagerly practice every kind of impurity. But that isn't what you <u>learned</u> about Christ. Since you have heard about Jesus and have <u>learned the truth</u> that comes from him, throw off your old sinful nature and your former way of life, which is corrupted by lust and deception. Instead, let the Spirit <u>renew your thoughts and attitudes.</u> Put on your new nature, created to be like God—truly righteous and holy.*

You were born to think like a man, in sin and depravity, but you've been born again to think like God.

We can't fight flesh with flesh, but I'm so glad that our weapons are not fleshly or carnal, but "mighty through God for the pulling down of strongholds" (2 Cor. 10:4). The people of God, the Spirit of God, and the Word of God are forever your allies.

THE TRUTH ABOUT YOU "IN CHRIST"

In this era of human history, you and I have the opportunity to experience a level of relationship with God that people never experienced through the entire Old Testament. There's a lot of doctrine in this chapter, but it's not just doctrine; it's doctrine that pulls our feelings up out of the valleys of deceit to the stable mountaintop of truth, and it's deeply personal doctrine for you. This dynamic relationship with the truth is about your personal relationship with Jesus Christ who IS the truth.

This doctrine is also so personal for God! His desire has always been that people be "In Christ."

2 Corinthians 5:17 (NKJV)
Therefore, if anyone is in Christ, he is a new creation; …

Compare your position in relationship to God to that of some of the giants of the Old Testament.

- Adam and Eve: they dwelled with God in the garden. Sin separated them from the Lord and He wasn't satisfied with that, so God paid for an upgrade. God already had a plan for our mess before we blew it. "The Lamb was slain before the foundation of the world." God made a plan for them, but that relationship would never be what it once was.

- Abraham: God said, "Abraham I'm going to bless you and people will always remember how I blessed you, but walk before Me and be My friend because I am your great reward." To hear "Walk before Me" is good but it's not the same as being "in Christ" … it's not close enough.

- Moses: Then along comes Moses and God says "I'm going to do something for the first time and reveal to you My name. Go tell Pharaoh that 'I AM' sent you." Furthermore, the Lord invited Moses to draw near and said, "I'm going to let My glory pass by you" such that Moses' face shone from the encounter. "Be near Me" is nice, but it's still not "in Christ" … not close enough.

- David: David said, "I want to build a place for Your Presence to dwell and we can worship You," and the Lord let David's son Solomon build it. A place for the Ark of the Presence was good …but it wasn't close enough.

- <u>Immanuel:</u> Then Immanuel came and dwelt among the people. That was even better…but it wasn't close enough.

- <u>Disciples:</u> Before the resurrection of Jesus the disciples were invited to "Come follow" Jesus, God in the flesh. They were even promised that He would make them fishers of men. Following Christ is close too … but it's not close enough for God. He had even more in mind.

Have you ever had the thought, *If I had only been alive in the Bible times?* These ARE the Bible times! The story is still unfolding.

Or maybe you've thought, *If I could have just seen Jesus in the flesh like the disciples did, that would have been so amazing. Then I'd not have the troubles and struggles I do now!"*

Those disciples walked closely with Jesus, but before the resurrection, they didn't have what you have now! God wants you "in Christ."

All of Biblical history and all of this doctrine is pointing to this relationship we can have. All of this chapter is not just *doctrinal*, it's deeply *personal* for you and for God. We don't overcome sin in order protect our beliefs. We overcome sin to protect a bond of relationship. <u>It is protected by faith in the truth.</u>

"Be careful how you talk to yourself, because you are always listening."

_____

JOSHUA FINLEY

09

THINKING FOR A CHANGE

In the world of technology, we are always being hit with the need to upgrade. Years ago, a friend of mine bought me an iPad (yes, I have great friends!) and then another friend gave me a $40 gift card to buy apps for my new tablet. As I was trying to figure out the new technology, I kept getting pop-up messages stating that before I could download apps, I needed to upgrade my software. These amazing applications were gifted to me—already paid for—but I couldn't have access to the apps until I upgraded my software.

Jesus, at 12 years old was able to baffle the brightest, most academic religious leaders. His parents lost him for a bit in the crowd of travelers, and found him back in the temple at Jerusalem, engaging these men in a level of conversation that astonished them. Still, even Jesus had to keep growing in wisdom: that is, "upgrading" His wisdom software.

Luke 2:52 (NIV)
And Jesus grew in wisdom and stature, and in favor with God and man.

Legendary UCLA basketball coach John Wooden said "It's what you learn after you know it all that counts!" If we're going to go from here to the finish line of our life in victory, we're going to need regular upgrades of our thinking. Often our current problem is our current thinking.

Romans 12:2 (NLT)
Don't copy the behavior and customs of this world, but let God transform you into a new person by changing the way you think. Then you will learn to know God's will for you, which is good and pleasing and perfect.

I love how it says "let God," because you and I cannot transform ourselves. Transformation is done by Him, by His grace, and by His power. Transformation of your life can't happen without a transformation of your thinking, and when your thinking gets connected to the wisdom of God, you are getting a divine upgrade that keeps you on a path to victory.

"Then you will learn to know God's will for you" … you wouldn't be reading this book if you didn't have a deep hunger to know God's will for you more clearly.

Proverbs 23:7 (NKJV)
For as he thinks in his heart, so is he.

Be careful how you talk to yourself, because you are always listening.

You are the preacher you listen to the most! The quality of your life is dictated by the quality of your thought life.

Salvation is both an event and a process. You are spirit, soul, and body, and the salvation of God impacts all three. Knowing how to talk to yourself in a way that doesn't sabotage an area of your life is critical to capturing and maintaining victory over hurts and habits and hang-ups.

Salvation is an event in the sense that your spirit is saved in the very moment you place your faith in Jesus Christ as Lord and Savior. In that event, you are instantly made perfectly righteous (in right standing) in God's sight: perfectly holy. Your spirit cannot be improved upon after that moment. Your spirit, which was dead and asleep, is awakened and is made alive and born again. The righteousness of Christ is put into your spirit in that moment, that event. You couldn't get any more "righteous" than you are.

While salvation of your spirit man is an event, the salvation of your soul (your mind, will, and emotions) is in progress. My spirit WAS saved, but the Bible makes clear that my mind, my will, and my emotions (the soul) ARE BEING saved through the sanctification process of the Holy Spirit's work in my life. Thankfully, the Holy Spirit is always looking to transform us as we say "yes" to His promptings.

One day the body WILL be saved. I'm so glad that we'll get to cash in the body we have right now for a glorified heavenly body when it's all said and done (and we all say "Hallelujah!" to that).

God's salvation touches every part of who we are, but our spirit WAS saved, our soul is BEING saved, and our body WILL be saved.

Because this is true, when I get saved, my IDENTITY changes immediately ("I'm a new person in Christ, old things have passed away, I am the righteousness of God in Christ," and more), but my MINDSET changes *progressively*.

A friend of mine was recently married for the first time, at the age of 52. His identity changed the moment the vows were sealed; he went from "single" to "married" the moment the ceremony was solemnized. The mindset of this single bachelor will take a while to change, however! To go from the "freedom" of single living to the responsibility and sacrifice that love requires inside covenant takes time to walk out in any marriage, much less one that started later in life.

Likewise, we have a new "upgrade" downloaded into our spirit the moment we are saved, but walking out that new pattern of thinking may take some time. Ephesians 1:1 says that the Lord has already "blessed us with every spiritual blessing in the heavenly places in Christ."

I've talked a lot about faith, truth, and thinking already in this book, because I cannot overstate the importance of it! When my mind gets renewed to a new pattern of thinking, new patterns that line up with the wisdom of God, wisdom that falls in line with what is already true in my spirit, then all of a sudden, I will begin to manifest the Kingdom of God in my life. I will experience the victory that He has already won for me.

Our thinking is a big deal!

It's impossible to think wrong and live right.

It's impossible for old patterns of thinking to produce new patterns of living.

Thankfully, because of a renewed mind, we don't have to take old mindsets into new seasons!

"What we know can keep us from what we need to know."
Bill Johnson

So, what is the process for transformational thinking that lines up with the wisdom of God?

DISCOVERING HOW TO THINK DIFFERENTLY

The word "discover" can be broken down this way: *dis* = "to remove" and *cover* = "covering." How do we remove the cover over our thinking in order to see the wisdom of God? When we remove that, we live the "Luke 2:52 lifestyle," growing in wisdom.

The Origin of Wisdom

Where did wisdom come from? When did it start? Listen to this great passage about God bringing forth wisdom, constantly having wisdom dwelling "at His side."

Proverbs 8:22-36 (NIV)

"The Lord brought me forth as the first of his works, before his deeds of old; I was formed long ages ago, at the very beginning, when the world came to be. When there were no watery depths, I was given birth, when there were no springs overflowing with water; before the mountains were settled in place, before the hills, I was given birth, before he made the world or its fields or any of the dust of the earth. I was there when he set the heavens in place, when he marked out the horizon on the face of the deep, when he established the clouds above and fixed securely the fountains of the deep, when he gave the sea its boundary so the waters would not overstep his command, and when he marked out the foundations of the earth. Then I was constantly at his side. I was filled with delight day after day, rejoicing always in his presence, rejoicing in his whole world and delighting in mankind.

Even before God created creation, He created wisdom. It can truly be said of wisdom that "It's older than dirt!" Wisdom was God's first creation because He knew we'd need it most! It's almost as if God pre-stocked the refrigerator for us. "I'm going to create these children and they are going to need this wisdom, so I will create it and have it all available for them even before they get there."

Be certain, before you need it, God's wisdom is available to you. Today. Tomorrow. And every day.

The Priority of Wisdom

Proverbs 4:7 (NKJV)

Wisdom is the principal thing; Therefore get wisdom.

That Hebrew word "principal" means several things: first in time (predated creation), first in order (there is no such thing as order in your life without God's wisdom), and first in rank. If you were to think of an organizational chart, the renewed mind with the wisdom of God is "commander in chief" and your feelings rank lower than private first class! How can we not make wisdom our highest pursuit?

It's easier to think your way and guide yourself into right feelings, than to feel your way into right thinking. So often we want to do it backwards and allow the feelings to drive the bus rather than seeking, apprehending and asserting the wisdom of God upon our thinking and letting that renewed mind drive the train. The mind renewed by the wisdom of God is the principal thing.

The Value of Wisdom

The wisest man who ever lived, Solomon, had something to say also about the value of wisdom.

> Proverbs 3:15 (NKJV)
> *She is more precious than rubies, And all the things you may desire cannot compare with her.*

Though it will cost you everything, get wisdom. There is a saying "If you think education is expensive, try ignorance." As a parent of young children looking ahead to the costs of education, those dollar figures can be intimidating, but what is more intimidating to me is the awful expense of lacking wisdom! Solomon says "I don't care what you have to do to keep growing in wisdom! Do it! Get more!" I'm not talking about academically going to college. This is an exhortation to pursue God.

Why does Solomon say that? Because basically every problem we have is essentially a wisdom problem! If there's a problem with my health, in my marriage or family, or with a relationship in the community, essentially these are wisdom problems. Financial struggles are not a bank problem or an account problem; these are wisdom problems. True wealth and honor always go with wisdom.

We've got to apply the wisdom of God in our day to day lives and situations! After I preach on Sunday I'm not asking myself how I did that day. I'm asking "How are we as God's people doing on Monday, Tuesday and on throughout the week? Are we laying hold of the wisdom and truth of God in a way where we are moving forward into the victory and destiny God intended?"

People came from around the world to get the wisdom of King Solomon, and everywhere wisdom went, blessing and expansion happened. Wisdom is always bringing increase.

Wisdom is so valuable because it teaches you to do the right thing at the right time in the right way. Don't we all want more of that?

One time, a factory in Kentucky shut down with an equipment problem. The whole assembly was stopped, all of the factory workers were sent home, and managers scrambled unsuccessfully to get things going. They checked out the mechanical conditions of every machine in the assembly line and couldn't find any source for the problem. With productivity at a standstill and losses mounting with every passing minute, the desperate owner sent his corporate jet to bring in a knowledgeable equipment specialist named Keith from out of state.

Keith arrived with a small bag of tools hanging on his belt and walked quietly through the plant, observing the pressure he was under to provide answers. Managers clung nearby, looking over his shoulder as he assessed the situation. First out of his tool kit was a simple wrench. He took off a small pressure gauge on the line and replaced it with a test gauge also from his tool bag. It turned out that all of the machines were fine. The entire operation had shut down simply because the pressure gauge was giving a false reading. The needle had gotten stuck, and with a new $20 gauge sending a new signal, the whole line of machines received the electronic go-ahead to begin operating again.

As the consultant quietly put his wrench back in the bag, the owner exclaimed, "That was *it*?" Lower level managers scattered to avoid the owner's fury for allowing such a small item to shut down his company.

Keith wrote up a bill, at which the owner was even more flabbergasted.

"You weren't in here but 15 minutes, and you're going to give me this huge bill?"

Keith took back the invoice and itemized the costs for more understanding:

1. *Pressure gauge: $20*
2. *Knowing about pressure gauges: $___* (the remaining balance)

Wisdom knows what to do at the right time.

God always has the wisdom you need for the current situation or moment. Life always has "stuff" come at us, and there is a temptation to believe that a solution doesn't exist for it. The lie says, "There's no way out! I'm defeated. I'll fall again. This problem in my life is unsolvable."

In the Kingdom of God, there is no such thing as an unsolvable problem, a battle you cannot win, or an unbeatable challenge. God always has a path forward through the stuff of life. This is true for you individually and for nations collectively. Every challenge and problem is a wisdom issue. Such is the value of wisdom!

It all boils down to a choice between God's wisdom or our own wisdom. We won't find God's wisdom by being impulsive or reckless, but by seeking the God of wisdom.

When you hear the self-talk saying, "You are stuck and there is no way out," come back at that with a declaration of faith that says "God, I thank You that You are going to teach me to do the right thing at the right time and in the right way!"

Job was a pretty smart guy, and he has this to say:

Job 28:1-2, 12-28 (NIV)
There is a mine for silver and a place where gold is refined. Iron is taken from the earth, and copper is smelted from ore…

"But where can wisdom be found? Where does understanding dwell? Man does not comprehend its worth; it cannot be found in the land of the living. The deep says, 'It is not in me'; the sea says, 'It is not with me.' It cannot be bought with the finest gold, nor can its price be weighed in silver. It cannot be bought with the gold of Ophir, with precious onyx or sapphires. Neither gold nor crystal can compare with it, nor can it be had for jewels of gold. Coral and jasper are not worthy of mention; the price of wisdom is beyond rubies. The topaz of Cush cannot compare with it; it cannot be bought with pure gold.

"Where then does wisdom come from? Where does understanding dwell? It is hidden from the eyes of every living thing, concealed even from the birds of the air. Destruction and Death say, 'Only a rumor of it has reached our ears.' God understands the way to it and he alone knows where it dwells, for he views the ends of the earth and sees everything under the heavens. When he established the force of the wind and measured out the waters, when he made a decree for the rain and a path for the thunderstorm, then he looked at wisdom and appraised it; he confirmed it and tested it. And he said to man, 'The fear of the Lord — that is wisdom, and to shun evil is understanding.'"

You can't even buy wisdom, he says. Finally, Job announced that it is out of a humble relationship with God that wisdom is born. Solomon reinforced that conviction when he described the source of wisdom:

> Proverbs 9:10 (NIV)
> *The fear of the Lord is the beginning of wisdom.*

The fear of the Lord is an awe and reverence for God. The moment that awe and reverence for God comes into my life and heart, wisdom begins to grow, because He is the source of it.

God told Solomon, "Ask Me for anything."

The request Solomon made in 1 Kings 3:9 in the original Hebrew language was for an "understanding heart" or "a listening heart." If we can, with God's help, develop a listening heart, everything else will fall into place.

When with humility and reverence for God we honor His Word, His Presence, and His people, wisdom comes into our lives. Our thinking gets an upgrade, and our life moves forward following the thinking.

YOU WERE BORN WITH A GOD-GIVEN DESIRE FOR WISDOM

Genesis 3:4-6 (NIV, underline added)
Then the serpent said to the woman, "You will not surely die. For God knows that in the day you eat of it your eyes will be opened, and you will be like God, knowing good and evil."
So when the woman saw that the tree was good for food, that it was pleasant to the eyes, and a tree <u>desirable to make one wise,</u> she took of its fruit and ate. She also gave to her husband with her, and he ate.

It's this pursuit of wisdom that trips us up in life and causes us to fall into sin. Having the desire isn't wrong. Going to the wrong person for wisdom is what sends us catapulting down the wrong and harmful path.

God put inside each of us a desire to be wise. The serpent always comes along and tries to get us to seek the fulfillment of that desire by going after our desire in the wrong time and in the wrong way, the opposite of wisdom.

THE TWO KINDS OF WISDOM

There is wisdom from above and there is wisdom from below. Isaiah put it this way:

Isaiah 55:8-9 (NIV)
"For my thoughts are not your thoughts, neither are your ways my ways,"
declares the Lord. "As the heavens are higher than the earth, so are my ways higher than your ways and my thoughts than your thoughts."

Sometimes people read those verses and treat it as if God is stating this in order to establish a huge gulf between us and Him, as if He's saying, "My ways are *SO* much higher than yours! Na-na, na-na, boo-boo, you can never think as high as I do!"

That's not what's happening at all! He is stating for us that on the path to overcoming, if His thoughts become our thoughts, then our ways will become His ways. Our thoughts and our ways are always connected!

If we are going to have an upgrade in our way of life, it must always be connected to an upgrade in our thinking, and His wisdom is the ultimate upgrade.

James said that the wisdom from above "is first pure, then peaceable, gentle, willing to yield, full of mercy and good fruits, without partiality and without hypocrisy." (See James 3:17.) God's wisdom is FULL of good fruit, meaning it always produces great things in our lives.

OUR ACCESS TO WISDOM

Paul made an incredible statement in 1 Corinthians 2:16, "But we have the mind of Christ." What an amazing declaration about every believer's inheritance!

You've heard the funny expression "living inside your head." In this case, living inside the mind of God is not a tease; it's a reality and a door of access into the mind, heart, and wisdom of God Himself!

People in the intelligence community of our governments will risk, and in some cases sacrifice, their very lives to obtain intelligence that will help their nation gain an advantage. Whether it's the NSA, the CIA, the FBI, or Homeland Security agents, classified information and top-secret intelligence files are the purview of only a select few individuals. When there is a violation of the terms of who can view certain information, or when there is a leak to the public of classified documents, people get in great legal trouble; on an international scale, it can jeopardize their very lives.

While people risk and sacrifice their lives to get government intel, Jesus sacrificed His life so that you and I could have access to the mind of Christ. It is not something that you have to obtain rights to through meeting a certain number of legalistic standards. In a sense, you already have "clearance" from heaven to obtain all the divine wisdom you need to solve problems and live an overcoming life.

We don't need government information! We want God's information, thoughts and divine wisdom to bring the power of the Kingdom of Heaven to bear upon our life circumstances and pathways. Jesus paid the price so that we could have access to that.

THE MIND OF CHRIST GOVERNING OUR LIVES?

Don't you love and hate the "autocorrect" functions on our latest technology? It can be a huge help or it can get you in trouble. It spews out what is programmed in.

One time my mom received a text from her friend Diane: *How are you doing, Shelly?*

My mom, struggling to use her ancient T9 technology on her phone, finally responded with this text: *"Oh we're doing great. The family is over and we're all smoking pot."*

Diane was confused, *"Shelly?"*

To this day, nobody knows what my mother intended to say, but that's what came out on her phone. My mom is a Godly woman who does not and will not ever smoke marijuana; however, the autocorrect function turned out a message all its own.

If we have access to the mind of Christ, the next challenge is to get it programmed into our minds so that the mind of Christ becomes the automatic response governing our lives.

Neuroscience is discovering amazing connections between this 3-pound, jelly-like substance that makes up the physical organ called "the brain," and the inanimate thinking called "the mind." There are over 200 billion nerve cells, or neurons, in the brain. The structure that permits a neuron to transmit signals from one nerve cell to another is called a synapse. There are over 125 trillion synapses in the cerebral cortex alone. The latest studies show that thoughts take up space, the brain has a capacity to grow, and new neurons can be added.

Think of the thoughts in our brain like trees standing in a forest; each thought takes up space like a tree takes up space in a forest. Negative thoughts like fear, anger, unforgiveness, and rejection actually damage the brain.

About 80% of our thoughts are subconscious and only 20% are conscious, so much of our conscious thinking is governed by the thoughts that are firmly planted in the unconscious "forest" of the mind.

Gaps and spaces in the brain can be replaced with either automatic negative thoughts or automatic positive thoughts. In this way, brains can either "auto self-destruct" or "autocorrect." When the mind takes in signals and information consciously, there are "auto responses" that are constantly at work behind the scenes.

The key to upgrading the software of our mind and resetting the auto-responses of our life is to reprogram the mind with the Word of God.

> Hebrews 4:12-13 (NIV)
> *For the word of God is living and active. Sharper than any double-edged sword, it penetrates even to dividing soul and spirit, joints and marrow; it judges the thoughts and attitudes of the heart.*

Spaces in the brain will be taken up by what we program in. What we program in will determine if we "auto correct" or "auto self-destruct." Recent studies show that if we use the brain correctly, new brain cells grow and new connections are made! New pathways and brain cells can be created as our thinking patterns change. Dr. Caroline Leaf said, "Science is starting to catch up to the Kingdom of God."

> **"I can't afford to have a thought in my head about me that God doesn't have in His."**
>
> BILL JOHNSON

We are going to have toxic thoughts. We are going to have feelings of fear and waves of guilt come over us. The question is, what will we renew our minds with? That determines what gets planted in the new spaces and what will help govern our ways. That's where we pray "God I want Your wisdom. I need Your thoughts."

Why not take God up on His offer of His mind and His thoughts? His thoughts are a word written down. When you read the Word of God, you are "getting inside God's head", utilizing your access to God's intel. If old patterns of thinking are bringing us down in lifestyle (and literally damaging our brain), then let's get off those dead horses and take up some new thoughts from God. There are millions of them to believe and choose from. It's a process of reprogramming the mind with His words and His thoughts, upgrading the software and auto-responses of our life.

I spend a lot of my time before God allowing His thoughts to wash over me, renewing my mind. In that subconscious forest of my brain, out of which so much of my life is governed, I'm planting and building a place where His wisdom reigns more and more.

APPLYING WISDOM TO WIN OUR BATTLES

Where are the battles in your life?

2 Corinthians 10:3-5 (KJV)
For though we walk in the flesh, we do not war after the flesh:

(For the weapons of our warfare are not carnal, but mighty through God to the pulling down of strong holds;) Casting down imaginations, and every high thing that exalteth itself against the knowledge of God, and bringing into captivity every thought to the obedience of Christ.

What is a stronghold? It's a continual pattern of thinking reinforced by lies contrary to the wisdom and truth of God. If you think of each thought as a tree in the forest of your mind, there are some trees or thoughts that need to be cut down. You may even need a prescribed burn in the forest of your mind, a forest fire to clear out some of the established tree-like thoughts that are standing in your brain.

Notice in that passage of scripture relating to warfare, the words "imaginations," "knowledge," and "thought." So, where is the battle for your victory? In your mind.

SIN'S CONCEPTION AND THE WISDOM THAT CONQUERS

God's wisdom provides a way out of sin, and James provides great insight.

James 1:13-15 (NIV)
When tempted, no one should say, "God is tempting me." For God cannot be tempted by evil, nor does he tempt anyone; but each person is tempted when they are dragged away by their own evil desire (lust) and enticed. Then, after desire has conceived, it gives birth to sin; and sin, when it is full-grown, gives birth to death.

Lust just means "strong desire." We use the word mostly to describe unholy sexual desires, but on its own, the word just means a strong desire in your flesh for something.

You can have a strong desire or lust for the Word of God.

James said we have temptation when two things are going on: a lust or strong desire in our flesh, and an enticement. My flesh intensely wants something and my mind is enticed!

James used the illustration of "conception" in verse 15; two things come together and give birth to sin. When presented with an opportunity to sin, guess what our flesh votes every time? A resounding "Yes!" In the same circumstance, what will my "spirit man" vote? A resounding "No" every time! The righteousness of God dwells and rules in my spirit; you cannot improve on that.

What will determine the outcome? My flesh says "Yes, please" and my spirit says "Don't even think about it!" My mind is the referee casting the deciding vote.

Just as in natural life, there is no conception of life without both a sperm and an egg. In the spiritual, there is no conception of sin without both the fleshly desire and the mind getting on board. James says further that when sin is conceived, it gives birth to death. Death and life come from the processes and battles of the mind.

Every type of sin (sexual sin, overspending, overeating, laziness, verbal abuse, anxiety and worry) is conceived when desire and enticement meet. When sin is conceived, death is birthed and our lives are mired in the sorrow of the consequences.

THINK WITHOUT LIMITS – GOD IS ABLE

God's ability is unlimited, and He has given us an imagination that can think without limits. Plant some new "trees" of God's wisdom and thought in the forest of your mind, and begin with this one: GOD IS ABLE.

A renewed mind planted with healthy trees of thought and wisdom begins with God's ability, not ours.

Ephesians 3:20-21 (NIV)
Now to him who is able to do immeasurably more than all we ask or

imagine, according to his power that is at work within us, 21 to him be
glory in the church and in Christ Jesus throughout all generations, forever
and ever! Amen.

Whenever I find my mind grappling with thoughts of failure and frustration, I pull out my seed bag and declare that I'm planting some new trees in my mind, thoughts that start with "God is able" and continue with "God is bigger than this" and I just keep planting.

We're discovering how to remove the lid off of our mind, and to seek and receive God's wisdom. If Jesus had to grow in wisdom, how much more can all of us keep receiving? More and more of the wisdom God has been made available to bring us into victory and wholeness.

Thankfully, the Bible says that if we lack it, we just need to ask for it. He's got plenty to give in abundance and He promises to provide it. And as 2 Timothy 1:7 says, "God has NOT given us a spirit of fear but of power, love, and a SOUND MIND." (emphasis added)

It all comes back to Jesus, because IN HIM is hidden every treasure of wisdom and knowledge you could ever desire or need. Let your imagination be used in thinking about God's nature, and the truth about the nature He put in you. Plant some seed, "God is able."

I want more of God's thoughts in my brain.

When I was 5 or 6 years old, I came running into a room and stopped cold because there was my Dad, on the phone. My Dad never touched the phone. Between my sisters monopolizing it and Dad avoiding it, this was a sight I had never seen before. He did a great job of keeping order in our home, but many times we saw him as a kind of sheriff. (I'm actually thankful for his approach to child rearing, because if not for that, several of us would probably not be alive.) The six of us drove him crazy, acting foolishly. Dad's hair never went gray. The tension that we kids created caused him to go from dark to stark white in his 30's.

Anyway, what caught me off guard was not only that Dad on the phone, but what I overheard him saying. Dad was talking to a friend about us. The words I heard him share in that moment were, "I just love them. They are such good kids."

I wondered, *Does Dad have another family? Who is he talking about?*

Thirty years later, those words still impact my life! Why? Because I was able to listen in on my father's thoughts.

When you open up the Word of God today, you have an opportunity to overhear your Father's thoughts about you. You may be feeling like such a failure, like you're such a lousy sinner, such a loser, stuck in a pit you can't get out of. Listen to your Father's thoughts! "I love My kids. Great kids. I have to discipline them and teach them, but I love them so much."

How you view yourself changes everything.

Let Him transform you into a new person by allowing Him to change the way you think.

Give Him the time, soaking in His Presence, opening up to His thoughts, so that you might think without limits. He's given you access to His thoughts. It's what you were born with a yearning for. Remember, it's what you learn after you know it all that counts and changes you.

"We fight from victory, not for it."

BILL JOHNSON[23]

10

AFTERWARDS:
THE BATTLE YOU FIGHT AFTER THE BATTLE YOU WIN

How do I want to close a book like this, with people for whom God has poured out so much grace to be free of "every sin that so easily entangles us?"[24]

Let's imagine together a campfire in my back yard with my family there, getting out the bug spray, stoking the coals, trying to keep my boys from becoming pyromaniacs, and chilling together. The conversation turns from typical campfire fun and stories to an eventual discussion of some timeless principles that I want my boys to know. Like a sports franchise preparing for upcoming games, I want to give my sons a scouting report on what to expect ahead. I know some things that await my sons in the future, even at times when I won't be with them. As best I can, I want to prepare them for what they are about to step into.

That's the conversation I want to have with you in this closing chapter.

VICTORY HAS CONSEQUENCES, EVEN FOR THE WISE

Life isn't about just what happens in the moment but what happens "afterward." What is the "recoil" or the "repercussions" of decisions we make?

I have a friend who is gluten intolerant, and he was telling me of his pizza cravings. He has to resist the urge to eat certain foods he loves such as pizza, and success varies. Despite his intolerance, and knowing the consequences that await, sometimes he just decides to yield to that craving and indulge in the cheesy taste of a delicious hot pizza loaded with all the toppings. It tastes awesome going down, but he pays the price in a terrible way—afterwards.

Sometimes you click "buy" while online shopping and then discover certain hidden service fees or shipping costs and you start to suffer from "buyer's remorse"—afterwards.

We all understand the principle that we will have to live with undesirable results after making poor decisions based on temporary feelings, but we rarely talk about the reality and battles we face even after we make wise choices.

There is a battle you fight even after the battle you win!

In the epic *The Lord of the Rings* tale, Gandalf the Grey is the father-figure type of wizard who is helping Frodo and his friends ("The Fellowship of the Rings") make their way toward a place called Mordor, which is like hell on earth, so that they can destroy a ring of power. On a treacherous path through the mines of Moria, they encounter this demon-like creature called a Balrog.

Gandalf powerfully confronts it in a cataclysmic scene. The fleeing group races across a stone bridge as this massive demonic beast with a fiery whip nears and prepares to destroy them all. Don't get religious on me as I continue the story, but indulge me as I call Gandalf "the good wizard. " Gandalf turns and speaks to the Balrog, plants his rod at a point on the bridge and issues this firm declaration: "YOU SHALL NOT PASS!" At that point where his faith was planted, the stone bridge crumbles beneath the beast and it begins to fall into the dark chasm-like abyss below, separating the fire-breathing Balrog from the good guys on the remaining section of bridge.

What happens next is as shocking as the incredible victory just secured. While all the good guys are taking a deep relaxing breath of relief, realizing that their friend Gandalf has just saved their lives, Gandalf turns to join them beyond the remaining portion of bridge, while the beast catapults towards the bottom. Just then, the last tip of the Balrog's fiery whip swings up one last time from below, catching Gandalf's foot and pulling the powerful and awesome hero down off the bridge and into the chasm with it.

If you watched the movie, one second you were celebrating with us—"Gandalf, you are the man! That 'You shall not stand' command was like Jesus casting out a demon!"—only to find yourself with us a moment later, shouting "Oh no!" (Thankfully, he re-emerges back into the story in the next installment. Spoiler alert if you haven't seen it.)

But there is a battle you fight … AFTER the battle you win and after even the wisest decisions.

You deal with the root issues of a food addiction, lose a bunch of weight, hit your goal, only to discover that you have four weddings to go to in one summer, complete with dinner parties and celebrations.

You get a promotion at work, get a raise, and gain new influence only to immediately encounter a fresh test of your integrity over financial decisions, or you butt heads relationally with another leader in the company.

The Holy Spirit prompts you to give a big financial gift to a charity, but then you have to fight off the regret as the pain of that financial gift is challenged by the car breaking down, the refrigerator going on the fritz, and a dental emergency striking all in the same week.

You honor God with your purity throughout years of singleness and temptation, waiting for a spouse, find and get married to terrific person in a great wedding celebration. Afterward, you discover that now you have to figure out how to live as a married person to that same spouse, and work out the process of "two becoming one!"

God intervenes and provides you with children in direct answer to prayer, but then after that happy breakthrough, you learn that there are health problems or learning disabilities with one of the children, or you have to learn the whole process of just raising "ordinary" children in a challenging culture!

There is always a battle you fight … after the battle you win!

I would love to sit around this campfire and tell my sons, "I wish that this principle were not true. I wish that once you won a battle, it was over with and Jesus took us home!"

Margaret Thatcher, the gifted former Prime Minister of Great Britain said, "You may have to fight a battle more than once to win it." I could add to that, "You will probably have to fight a battle right after you just won one."

DO YOU WANT TO GET WELL?

I believe that this is the principle behind the seemingly strange question Jesus asked a paralyzed man at the Pool of Bethesda: "Do you want to be well?" Why wouldn't he want to get better? The man suffered with this infirmity for exactly 38 years, according to Scripture. Who wouldn't want Jesus to end that long bout of suffering? But what is "after" the healing?

The question strikes at the heart of "Are you willing to fight the new battles that will come after you're healed, the battles you've never fought before?" Would the man know and be willing to learn how to live and work rather than accept the alms given him as a beggar? Would he be willing to learn the life of living responsibly for himself, rather than being taken care of?

There is always a new battle to fight after the battle you win. While your soul is screaming to you about the battle you've been facing and the struggles you've had, have you thought beyond the guilt and shame to what life will look life after you've entered your "win" and start taking your "victory lap" around the stadium of life? There will be no cheering crowds in that day, only a new battle to face, and not just one. There will be another and another for the rest of our lives, because every new season brings new challenges.

VULNERABLE BUT VICTORIOUS

Victory makes you vulnerable. Promotion puts a target on your back. Every league in sports provides teams the opportunity to win the 1st Place Trophy along with that elusive label we call "Champion"— but then comes next year. Everybody wants to beat the defending champion. Every team is psyched up to play their best against the defending champs. Back to back repeat champions are very rare in sports for that reason. It's human nature after winning a big battle to take a vacation and go to Disneyland.

There's an important distinction between celebrating and letting down our guard. We should celebrate every victory God gives us, every battle over sin, every triumph. God is a celebratory God. Feasts in the Old Testament were often remembrances of great victories for the people of God. If we let down our guard, however, either spiritually or internally, we can set ourselves up for difficulty in the next battle.

I would tell my sons in this campfire chat that I never want them to live paranoid, but I want them to be *prepared*. I want them, and you, to live courageously, but also to be ready and aware.

The good news is that Jesus equips us with grace for every battle to overcome every challenge, but we still have to face them. If the Apostle Paul was also sitting around our campfire, he'd say "we are familiar with the devil's evil schemes."[25]

You were born into a fight.

"Josh, I'm not looking for a fight; I just want to beat this sinful habit I'm so ashamed of. I don't really want to get into another one. I'm a peaceful person."

The truth is that you were born into a fight, into kingdoms in conflict, and your adversary doesn't fight fair.

> "We fight from victory, not for it."
> **Bill Johnson**

I said those words from author and leader Bill Johnson to a young high school wrestler God brought into my life, named Brandon. This young son in the faith heard that and said "Pastor Josh, I get it!" He proceeded to tell me of a tournament his wrestling team was in with several schools, in which he was in the final match of the day. His coach counted the points from all the earlier matches, did the math, and realized that no matter what happened to Brandon in the final match, even if he got pinned, the team was guaranteed to walk away from the day with a team victory.

The coach pulled this young athlete aside and said "I just want to let you know, that no matter what happens with you in this last match of the day, our team will still win." What courage that instilled in him! There was no fear of "blowing the tournament for the whole team," and no fear of undermining the points his teammates had put on the board. Brandon still had to face his opponent, but totally free of pressure. This high school boy could face his opponent with a heart so full of courage knowing that even if he lost, he still won.

Without fear of failure, you can face your battles with courage and peace!

Likewise, the devil knows that he has lost the war in your life, but he wants to injure or even cripple God's warriors if he can. Jesus has already defeated him for you and given you the victory, but you still have to face him. The nice thing is that you face him as a victor. You can lose a skirmish but our King Jesus has won the war. There need be no fear of failure percolating in your heart and thoughts.

WHY MUST WE FIGHT BATTLES IF WE CAN'T LOSE THE WAR

It seems perhaps illogical for a system to be in place that requires us to fight temporal battles if the long term, eventual outcome has already been settled by Jesus Christ.

Oh, but there are so many benefits to battling these things. Battles are not pointless!

Battles bring rewards, both earthly and eternal.

Battles bring revelation to us about who we are, and who God is!

Battles draw attention to our testimonies, and bring glory to God when we lay hold of His grace to defeat the enemy. People watch your life when you go through battles and they recognize your faith in the God who is with you and they see how Jesus brings you through things into victory. This draws them to the Lord and brings Him glory!

Early in the book of Judges, it says that there were enemies still left in the Promised Land after Joshua's conquests and death. These were left to test Israel, and to teach those who had never experienced war, how to fight.

One of the most incredible and brilliant people I've ever met is a man named Elliot Tepper, who launched Betel (Spanish version of Bethel, meaning "house of God"), a ministry to the marginalized and impoverished, with shelters and recovery centers in over 25 countries. Elliot graduated from Harvard. With a call to serve God, he then attended and graduated from Elim Bible Institute, before launching into a lifetime of rescuing souls from the globe's gutters.

Recently, Elliot said to me, "Josh, man's greatest need is to know his need."

Battles put us into position where we more readily recognize our need. The goal in any battle is not to be focused on the tactics of our enemy, but to be fixated on trusting our God. I don't want you or anybody to be paranoid of our enemy's strategies, but I want you prepared to stay focused and to move forward into greater and greater victory.

What is our biggest need, whether the battle is spiritual, financial, marital, parental, emotional, or addictive behavior and hang-ups? The biggest need before, during, and after every battle, is to be totally dependent on Jesus.

"Continual dependency" is my constant strategy for life. Christ equips me for every battle the world, the flesh, and the devil have to throw at me.

FIVE BATTLES WE ALL MUST BE PREPARED TO WIN

Battle # 1 | Freedom

Noah, my hero, won an incredible battle, breaking free from a 100-year trial. He built an ark when it had never rained; people thought he was crazy. He was the only righteous person on the planet. The Bible says that every other person and family on the earth was wicked and unrighteous. That is a rough neighborhood to live in! That's a hostile environment! No small group Bible study for support, nobody singing worship songs with you, no Christian TV or radio to switch to with the remote, and no smörgåsbord of churches to pick from!

He passed this incredible test before facing a new one. After obediently building the ark and succeeding, he then had to climb into this boat and weathered the worst storm to ever strike mankind. On the ark were two of every kind of animal, his wife, three sons and three daughters in-law. What are you going to do on the boat that long? You can only play "I spy" so many times, and there was no motor on this ship to give you the option to have a little fun waiting it out.

There is a battle to fight after the battle you win. Noah won these incredible challenges of faith, but after winning those battles, what did he do with his newfound freedom? When he got back on the land, there was a new challenge, the "battle of freedom."

> Genesis 9:18-21
> *The sons of Noah who came out of the boat with their father were Shem, Ham, and Japheth. (Ham is the father of Canaan.) From these three sons of Noah came all the people who now populate the earth.*
> *After the flood, Noah began to cultivate the ground, and he planted a vineyard. One day he drank some wine he had made, and he became drunk and lay naked inside his tent.*

Of course, some bad things happened because of Noah's loss of this battle. There is always a battle you fight after the battle you win!

The battle of freedom is one that we face in every transition out of a structured environment. People sometimes do well in a structured rehabilitation center but struggle when their rehab stint is over.

Every college freshman faces this challenge after winning the battle of graduating high school, facing new decisions and choices that have never been faced before.

That's why parenting is not about rules and compliance, but about preparing people for freedom.

People I've walked with and loved have arrived at annual sobriety milestone days, and ironically don't know how to celebrate a milestone in any way but with drugs, alcohol, or sexual promiscuity, and lose this battle they faced after the earlier battle they won. Close friends of mine have lost family members to this battle.

Some people function well and thrive in strict or high-pressure work environments, but when given leave or free time, fumble the test of freedom.

Noah won incredible battles, but lost the battle of freedom.

How do we prepare ourselves for these battles of freedom? Remind ourselves of three things:

Reminder #1: "Where the Spirit of the Lord is there is freedom" (2 Cor. 3:17). In other words, I don't have to get AWAY from the Lord to FIND freedom. I need to stay CLOSE to Him so that I can live IN it.

Reminder #2: I remind myself of Psalm 16 "the boundary lines have fallen for me in pleasant places; surely I have a delightful inheritance." I don't have to look over the boundaries wondering if there is something better on the other side; I'm thankful for what is within the boundaries that my parents, bosses and others have put me under. All I need is within them.

Reminder #3: We must remind ourselves that God is not keeping things FROM us, but He's keeping things FOR us. "It was FOR freedom, Christ has set us free." God wants you and I free more than you want to be free. He wants us free more than any other being in the universe!

Battle # 2 | Fatigue

Elijah fought and won incredible battles. It was a very different era than Noah, but like Noah he lived in an ungodly culture. No matter what you think of our current political leadership here in our nation, we have nothing to complain about compared to Elijah. We don't have King Ahab and Queen Jezebel ruling and reigning in the level of wickedness they promoted.

Elijah lived victoriously in intense battles. He called down fire from heaven just to protect himself from the "secret service" that had been sent from the palace to kill him. Then there was that amazing day on Mount Carmel! In a hostile environment of idolatry and persecution of the righteous, he challenges the nation with the question:

> I Kings 18:21
> *"How long will you waver between two opinions? If the Lord is God then follow Him. If Baal is god, then follow him."*

Elijah was full of courage. There was no rain in the land for years by his prophetic command. He even had the audacity in the middle of a drought when water was scarce, to command servants to gather buckets of water and drench the sacrifices, fill up ditches and with the excess water being poured out. This guy had guts in the battles. He not only called down fire on the altar which consumed the sacrifice to God, but then took the opportunity to kill 450 false prophets of Baal.

That's one crazy, victorious day! But the day wasn't over yet. After the battles he won, there was one more battle for Elijah to face, the battle of fatigue:

1 Kings 19:1-4
When Ahab got home, he told Jezebel everything Elijah had done, including the way he had killed all the prophets of Baal. 2 So Jezebel sent this message to Elijah: "May the gods strike me and even kill me if by this time tomorrow I have not killed you just as you killed them."
3 Elijah was afraid and fled for his life. He went to Beersheba, a town in Judah, and he left his servant there. 4 Then he went on alone into the wilderness, traveling all day. He sat down under a solitary broom tree and prayed that he might die. "I have had enough, Lord," he said. "Take my life, for I am no better than my ancestors who have already died."

Former President Bill Clinton once said, "Most of the mistakes in my political and personal life are connected to sleep deprivation." That may sound like a cop-out, but truthfully, fatigue is a real factor in winning battles. There is a battle you fight after the battle you win.

> **"Tired eyes rarely see a good future."**
>
> MIKE MURDOCK

As Hall of Fame football coach Vince Lombardi said, "Fatigue can make cowards of us all." Elijah was clearly not a coward, but he was emotionally, spiritually, and physically depleted. He was human. Alone and afraid, Elijah cowered in the wilderness just 24 hours after winning some of the most courageous battles of faith ever recorded in Scripture.

> "As margin decreases, temptation increases."
> **Craig Groeschel**

If fatigue goes unchecked, fear and anxiety run rampant and can lead to bizarre decisions in the heat of tension.

What are some reminders to help us in the "Battle of Fatigue"?

First, remember that if the devil can't get you tripped up in being really bad, he'll settle for keeping you really busy, because he knows where that road leads to.

Remember, too, that sin looks more enticing when our souls are weary.

Third, remember the words of Jesus, "Take My yoke upon you, … and you will find rest" (Matthew 11:29).

And fourth, remember the words of Psalm 23: "He makes me lie down in green pastures. He restores my soul." In other words, "Get over here. Come close to Me, My sheep. Lie down and rest, so I can restore your soul!" Why? So that we can have courage and grace for what is ahead, the battle we face after the battle we win.

Battle # 3 | Forgetfulness

Joshua, the amazing general, survived and won the most amazing battle, the battle of a lifetime! Jericho was an intimidating, fortified, locked up city with seemingly impregnable and 40-foot- high-walls, considered impossible to get into. Joshua knew this was a battle that he could not win, so he inquired of the Lord. God's instructions were clear: march around the walls for six days, and then march around again seven times on the seventh day, not doing or saying anything. This was clearly a supernatural victory.

Next town on the conquest list was a little place called Ai.

Joshua 7:2-5 (NLT)

Joshua sent some of his men from Jericho to spy out the town of Ai, east of Bethel, near Beth-aven. When they returned, they told Joshua, "There's no need for all of us to go up there; it won't take more than two or three thousand men to attack Ai. Since there are so few of them, don't make all our people struggle to go up there."

So approximately 3,000 warriors were sent, but they were soundly defeated. The men of Ai chased the Israelites from the town gate as far as the quarries, and they killed about thirty-six who were retreating down the slope. The Israelites were paralyzed with fear at this turn of events, and their courage melted away.

You can't treat every battle the same way. Each one is unique.

Or sometimes you brace yourself for these big seasons and big battles, and then the small foxes that the Bible speaks of come in.

Having lived in Western New York for many years, I became familiar with the story of a circus performer and stuntman named Bobby Leach. Bobby was the second person to ever survive a trip over Niagara Falls in a barrel in 1911, and only the first man. After his stunt, he spent six months in the hospital recovering from two broken kneecaps and a fractured jaw, but he lived! Until 1926, that is. That was the year he slipped on an orange peel while in New Zealand and injured his leg. Gangrene set in and the leg had to be amputated. Sadly, he died of complications to the surgery. Bobby Leach survived Niagara Falls in a barrel in a great stuntman's victory over fear, but lost to an orange peel!

We must do things God's way to get God's result. It matters that we listen to the Holy Spirit. He wants to protect us and guide us and lead us in wisdom. In the battle of Jericho, God said, "Take no spoils," but Achan decided to do things his own way and took some. His failure to listen and obey cost the whole nation in the next battle. The great battle and victory of Jericho was followed by the loss at Ai, because of a few trinkets squirreled away by one person who wasn't ready for the battle you fight after the one you win.

When we win a battle, or receive a blessing, we have to remind ourselves where it came from. There's no need to "help God" bless you. All things come FROM Him, it all flows THROUGH Him, and it's all going to go BACK to Him.

Spiritual amnesia results from winning a battle and then forgetting how it happened. There is a rhythm that a warrior son or daughter of God lives in, remembering some important truths.

First of all, Jesus said in John 15, "Without Me you can do nothing." When we look back over our shoulder and see the victories that we've won, the compliments that we've received from others, the "thank-yous" for a job well done, we can turn back to the Father, lift all of that up to Him at the end of the day, and give Him thanks because any good thing we've accomplished came from Him.

Secondly, I'll say this again: Constant dependency is our continual strategy. What's my strategy for spiritual warfare? My strategy is not focusing on the enemy or his tactics at all, but worshiping God and trusting in God all the time. Worship is our act of spiritual warfare.

Thirdly and so importantly, it's less about having my defenses up against my enemy and more about having my guard down towards my Father. If we trust Him, we can say "yes" again and again.

Battle # 4 | Familiarity

So valuable to the nation of Israel was the "Ark of the Covenant," the approximately 2' x 4' golden box that housed the manifest Presence of God. The nation was blessed for having it.

One day the Philistines captured it from Israel in battle, a devastating defeat for the nation. This was a headline-making tragedy for Israel; the Ark of God

Almighty was in their enemy's hands.

For the nation whose unique identity was woven into its relationship with the Lord, nothing was more important that recovering the Ark of God. How would they win it back? Find a better battle strategy? How many lives would it cost to fight again, hoping to win?

What the Philistines were shocked to discover was that this Ark was not just some kind of lucky charm. Having it in their possession didn't have the result that they hoped for. When you put the manifest Presence of God amidst idol worship, it's not going to fit in very well. Instead of bringing them even more fortune, the Philistines began to discover that the Ark was not a blessing for them at all, but a curse.

Without the Israelites even having to go to battle or kill anybody to recover their beloved Ark of God's Covenant, the Philistines just "sent it back." What a God-given victory as the oxen came pulling the cart and the Ark back to Israel with no military skirmish or escort!

Back in Israel the Ark of the Covenant was placed, kept and cared for at the house of a man named Abinadab.

Years later, in sorrow that the Ark of God's manifest Presence was not in Jerusalem at the place of worship, David commissioned some men to bring it from Abinidab's house to the place prepared for it in the City of David. Along the way however, there was a problem.

2 Samuel 6:5-7 (NLT)
David and all the people of Israel were celebrating before the Lord (30,000 of his best troops), singing songs and playing all kinds of musical instruments—lyres, harps, tambourines, castanets, and cymbals.

But when they arrived at the threshing floor of Nacon, the oxen stumbled, and Uzzah reached out his hand and steadied the Ark of God. Then the Lord's anger was aroused against Uzzah, and God struck him dead because of this. So Uzzah died right there beside the Ark of God.

Honestly, that sounds just a little harsh, doesn't it? I mean, Uzzah is just trying to keep the most important relic to the nation from crashing down to the ground!

God is not unjust or unloving, however. These kinds of things don't just happen unless there's a heart issue that He's aware of.

What we can easily miss in the story is that Uzzah is one of Abinidab's sons. He and his brother Ahio had grown up for years with the Ark of the Covenant in their home. Being around the Ark was not unfamiliar to them!

After the nation won the battle of recovering the Ark without a fight, Uzzah lost the next battle, the Battle of Familiarity. The Ark was more than just a piece of furniture. It was not an idol or a good luck charm. It was the very Presence of the God of the universe.

Have you ever lost the Battle of Familiarity? Have you ever begun to treat something with less value because it's so common to you? Of course you have! We have parents, spouses, children and people in our lives that we are so used to, that we can easily treat them with less value than they are given by God.

Have you treated your God-given position as His child with too much familiarity? Have you treated holiness with too much familiarity? In the Old Testament, God's Presence was housed in a box. In the New Testament, God's Presence is housed within our bodies. Have you taken that for granted or failed to see the glory that rests upon you and upon one another?

Have you treated the opportunity to connect with His Presence in the Word with too much familiarity? We want to be a "friend of God" without becoming "familiar" with God. I don't want to be afraid of Him or come with trepidation; I want to be His friend. But I also want to treat Him with the awe, majesty, and holiness that He deserves. Familiarity breeds contempt. If unchecked, familiarity causes me to forget something's value.

Battle # 5 | Favor

"Favor from heaven can cause problems on earth."
Bill Johnson

When favor comes upon your life, a battle ensues!

Jesus Himself had to battle this one after He had won other battles. He lived a perfect, sinless life, and experienced the favor of God and had favor with man. He lived His 30 years of training for ministry flawlessly. He was gracious towards people and sensitive to God the Father. He was "God in the flesh." At Jesus' water baptism in the Jordan River by John, the heavens ripped open, the Spirit of God descended, and He heard the audible voice of God saying, "This is My Son (affirmation), whom I love (affection), in Him I am well pleased (approval)."[26]

Then the Spirit led Him into the wilderness. He fasted and was tested by the devil.

"If you are the Son of God, turn these stones into bread (security).
If You are the Son of god, jump down from there (safety).
If you will bow down and worship me, I will give you the kingdoms of this world (significance)."[27]

The enemy tempted Jesus to find His security, His safety, and His significance in things other than His identity and relationship with the Father. The enemy will try the same tactics on us. The enemy always attacks your identity, because if he can get you thinking that you're someone that you're not, he can get you behaving in a way that you were never created to live.

Even Jesus had battles to fight after the battle He won. After winning a 30-year battle flawlessly and growing in favor with God and man, even hearing the audible approval of the Father, He then had another battle to fight.

How does God's favor on your life create a battle? With every favor comes victory and blessing, but with every blessing comes the weight of that burden. With victory comes responsibility because favor from heaven can cause problems on earth. You win a victory and suddenly those around you are envious, doubtful, or critical. You encounter resistance after a victory.

Luke 4:13 (NLT)
When the devil had finished tempting Jesus, he left him until the next opportunity came.

It doesn't say that he left Jesus alone for good, but that there would be another battle on another day! There is a battle to fight after the battle you win, but because Jesus Himself faced this, He can help you win every single battle you face!

Jesus can help you win *every* battle. He knows what's coming at you before it comes. He doesn't want you paranoid, but He wants you prepared.

THREE TAKEAWAYS FROM THIS CAMPFIRE CHAT

1 | Be Kind to People
Everyone we meet is fighting a battle that we know nothing about. Each person has a story of life battles that we've never heard. People are affected by our progress in the battles we face, and we are affected by theirs, but we can't presume to understand their temptation, their responses, their motives, or their actions. Nobody saw David fighting the lion and the bear, and we don't see the battles others are in. Be kind, always.

#2 | We Fight FROM Victory, Not FOR It
Never forget it! Jesus did a lot more than we can sometimes remember.

The Holy Spirit often speaks to me in baseball analogies, because I am a baseball lover despite the fact that many think baseball is a boring sport. Unlike soccer or hockey where the action never stops, or football where every play matters, when watching baseball, I can sit back, relax, order another hot dog, and eat more food. No wonder it is "America's Pastime."

Here's the illustration: Jesus already hit the home run. Our life is entirely wrapped up in running around the bases for Him and in His honor. I didn't hit the home run; He did!

When we're faced with a battle, we must remind ourselves that "I can't lose!" The enemy may pin you to the mat for a moment, but in Christ you're still going to win.

3 | Constant Dependency is Our Continual Strategy
How do I overcome to win life's battles in every area?

We never outgrow our need for more of Jesus. A man's greatest need is to know his need. Maturing into greater childlikeness or childlike dependency is the way of the Kingdom of God. As sons and daughters, we can never forget the source. Surrender to the Lord is our safest place.

I love the lyrics to the song "I Need You More:"[28]

I need You more, more than yesterday
I need You Lord more than words can say
I need You more than ever before
I need You Lord. I need You Lord

More than the air I breathe
More than the song I sing
More than the next heartbeat
More than anything
And Lord as time goes by
I'll be by Your side
Cause I never want to go back
To my old life

Right here in Your presence is where I belong
This old broken heart has finally found a home
And I'll never be alone

God gives grace to the humble but resists the proud. Have you reached a milestone, or are you coming off a huge victory or heading off to a new venture and season in life? Humble yourself before the Lord and recognize that there are more battles coming. Surrender yourself afresh.

And when you trip up in the days ahead, just remember that failure is not final. Every morning we get new mercy. That's how it works; new morning, new mercy. Part of overcoming is realizing that it is a lifestyle & mindset, not just a momentary victory.

So, my friend...

Embrace God's boundaries.

Take your stand.

Don't walk alone.

Embrace the victory coming your way.

Remember that you live under the smile of heaven.

Overcome.

ACKNOWLEDGEMENTS

There are so many people in my life I'd like to take a moment to sincerely thank from the bottom of my heart. To my wife, **Anna**, you represent the grace, wisdom, and mystery of God in my life more than you could ever imagine. To our boys, **Judah & Jesse**, you are world-changers, history-makers and men of God! To my writer, **Jack Hempfling**, your heart for Jesus and people is a continual inspiration. This book would not have happened without your belief and hard work! To **Josh Mitchell** for all of your technical expertise and amazing personal support! To my editor, **Kim Leach**, you embody the definition of "love is patient and kind!" To my graphic designer and spiritual daughter, **Chelsea Phillips**, your creativity is a gift and a weapon—you are powerful! To the **Elim Gospel Church** community who walked with us in our first 15 years of ministry and training, your love and maturity has invested incredible treasures into our family! We will forever be grateful for your trust and support. To our pastors, **Wade & Dawn Haskins**, and to our **Freedom Church family**, your acceptance of us and your commitment to growing emotionally healthy Christ-followers is truly second to none. To our parents on both sides of the family (**Raymond, Michele, Richard & Lori**) your love has made us who we are today. You led us to Jesus and showed us what it meant to offer Him a fresh "yes" in every season. To my five siblings (**Michael, Laurie, Kathy, Matthew and Jenny**) thank you for never taking me too seriously as a minister, not letting me forget where I've come from and still celebrating all that Jesus is doing in and through me. To my spiritual father, **Eric Peoples**, you are a true disciple-maker; you saw value in me and have not stopped calling out the gold in me for the past 25 years! To my best friend, **Tariq Shah**, you are a friend that sticks closer than a brother. To **Dick & Debbie Slakes** for modeling what an enduring marriage looks like, just wow. To **all of my friends** who have and are in the process of overcoming an addiction, you are my heroes! You have given me a real-life reminder that grace is more powerful than sin. And to **Jesus**, Who paid the ultimate price for my freedom and who reminds me daily that I live under the smile of Heaven, You are the original Overcomer that I worship and follow.

ENDNOTES

Chapter 2

1   Johnson, B. (2006). *Dreaming with God.* Shippensburg, PA: Destiny Image Publishers, Inc. 26.

2   Sheets, D. (2017). *Roll Away Your Stone.* Bloomington, MN: Bethany House Publishers.

3   Proverbs 24:16

Chapter 3

4   Glen Berteau. "One More Night with the Frogs". The House. Modesto, CA. September 6, 2016.

Chapter 5

5   Paul Manwaring, "Shame: The Ultimate Identity Theft," Paul Manwaring: Fathering Poeple & Organisations (blog), November 11, 2014, https://paulman-

waring.com/2014/11/11/shame-the-ultimate-identity-theft/

6   *Shrek.* Directed by Andrew Adamson and Vicky Jenson. Based upon the book by William Steig. Glendale, CA: DreamWorks, 2001.

7   TED. (2012, March 16). *Listening to shame | Brene Brown* [Video file]. Retrieved from https://youtu.be/psN1DORYYV0

8   Matthew 5:18

9   John 3:16

10   Scanlon, Paul. "All those former Versions of you would like to thank for not mistaking them as the final you.
They don't miss you, need to hear from you nor do they want you to visit or go back for a vacation... it's all good." Facebook, 19 July. 2019, https://www.facebook.com/PaulScanlonUK/photos/all-those-former-versions-of-you-would-like-to-thank-for-not-mistaking-them-as-t/2912431515497338/

Chapter 6

11   TEDx Talks. (2010, October 6). *The power of vulnerability | Brene Brown | TEDxHouston* [Video file]. Retrieved from https://youtu.be/X4Qm9cGRub0

12   Genesis 39:8 (NLT).

13   Reccord, B. (2002). *Beneath the Surface.* Nashville, TN: Broadman & Holman Publisher. 73-75.

14   Stanley, A. (2003). The Next Generation Leader. Colorado Springs, CO: Multnomah Books. 153.

Chapter 7

15   Laurie Bolton. Elim Fellowship WINGS Training. Elim Gospel Church. Lima, NY. January 2016.

16   Hybels, B. (2008). *Axiom.* Grand Rapids, MI: Zondervan. 101.

17   Miller, D. (2006). *Scary Close: Dropping the Act and Acquiring a Taste for True Intimacy.* Nashville, TN: Nelson Books.

Chapter 8

18   Galatians 3:3

19   gatewaychurchtv. (2014, October 24). Past.....Present....Future [Video file]. Retrieved from https://youtu.be/7pWAmj9fkqI

20   2 Corinthians 2:14

21   Matthew 10:16

22   1 Corinthians 14:1

23   Johnson, Bill. "Principles of Warfare". Bethel Church Sermon of the Week. Podcast audio, February 3, 2019. https://www.bethel.tv/en/podcasts/sermons/episodes/322

Chapter 10

24   Hebrews 12:1

25   2 Corinthians 2:11

26   Matthew 3:17; Chris Hodges. ARC GROW Conference. Las Vegas, NV. September 2017.

27   Matthew 4:3,6,9, parentheses added by author

28   Lindell Cooley, Bruce Jerry Haynes, "I Need You More". (1996). Centergy Music / Integrity's Hosanna! Music.

CLAIM YOUR **FREE** BONUSES
AT READOVERCOME.COM/BONUS!

Exclusive author videos, resources, and more!

JOSHUAFINLEY.ORG

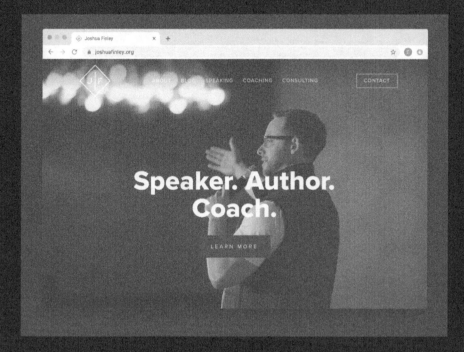

Visit joshuafinley.org for more resources!

Blogs
Speaking
Coaching
Consulting
Store

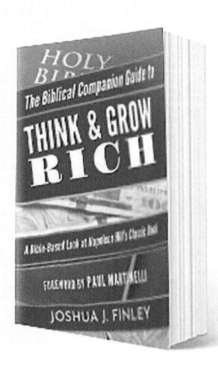

NEW BOOK!

The Biblical Companion Guide to THINK & GROW RICH by Joshua Finley

DIGITAL COURSE

Get lifetime access to the Think & Grow Rich digital course today and discover how your thinking can lead to greater breakthroughs!

- *Watch as many times as you like in your private membership portal*
- *Lifetime access to 16+ teaching videos*
- *3 bonus video sessions on "The 3 Missing Chapters"*
- *Audio versions of each daily lesson to download and listen on-the-go*
- *Access to 6 Facebook LIVE sessions (lifetime access!)*
- *1 growth sheet to complete every day*
- *Q&A/Sharing sessions*
- *Digital Flipbook of the original version of* Think & Grow Rich
- *PDF version of* Think & Grow Rich
- *Access to the members-only program portal (watch again & again)*
- *Access to membership app for easy content access*
- *Access to our private Facebook group*

Visit joshuafinley.org/store for more!

AUTHOR ACADEMY elite

DO YOU DREAM OF WRITING A BOOK?

✓ Gain credibility and influence

✓ Impact people around the world

✓ Create a lasting legacy

✓ Earn passive income

✓ Spread your message

✓ Experience new opportunities

✓ Travel to interesting places

✓ Meet new people

AUTHORACADEMYELITE.COM